LOVE
FEARLESSLY

The Soulmate Within

Love,
Kristen

KRISTEN LILLIAN SCHNEIDER

First Printing: 2019
ISBN 978-1-64516-305-3
www.wellblends.com

Cover and Book Interior Design by: Najdan Mancic, Iskon Design
Author's Portraits by: The Leonardo

Contents

"Fear knocked at the door. Faith answered. No one was there."

—*Proverb*

INCEPTION ...

I WAS NINE years old. I was sitting cross-legged in the attic loft of my parents home. It was late. The rest of the house was fast asleep. My caramel hair was wrapped up in a messy bun stacked on top of my head. I was in cotton shorts and a pink tank top. My hands were clammy. I stared at the cursor as the computer screen flickered rapidly. *I am not writing this for you. I am writing this for me. I have two characters within me; one on each shoulder. One sounds like the devil. The other like an angel. I don't know which one to believe.* That's all I wrote. Then I deleted it, and I continued to stare at the rapid flicker on the oversized Macintosh computer screen. I didn't know then that these characters that were apparent to me even as a child were the representations of fear and love that exist within each of us. On some subconscious level, I must have recognized that these two dueling themes did, and would always, reside inside of me. Unbeknownst to me at the time, I was about to spend decades, not in years, but in significant moments of experience, hours of research, and months of reflection trying to sort out just what the angel of love and the devil of fear represented in my life and the overall picture of humanity.

CHAPTER ONE

Author's Story

I AM NOT a therapist. I am not a master. I'm not an official researcher, nor do I have a Ph.D. I don't have a ton of letters behind my name or a lofty list of accolades. What I am is a woman who has lived a life littered by the unwelcomed intrusion of fear. I have reached my threshold. I am a woman who wants to silence any voice, particularly my own, that makes me feel less than. I am a woman who has embarked upon a mission to understand, dismantle, and overcome unnecessary pain. Let's be clear, I am writing this for myself. This is an exercise in catharsis. It is my hope, and perhaps optimistic delusion, that this will be of some value to someone else. To you my dear reader, I shall call you a friend. So friend, I thank you for holding these pages in your hand and for being with me now. Much of what I have to say has come in the form of revelations and dare I say, epiphanies. The rest of it, while it has been meditated upon, is not premeditated and will be hashed out in real time as my fingers tinker across this keyboard. While I have been graced with the good fortune of discovering profound answers and valid tools, I also pose questions that remain for the time, unanswered.

I live by in large by Socrates' conviction, "The unexamined life is not worth living." While the life of a seeker is pregnant with curiosity and layers of deep thoughts, I try to keep a good sense of humor about the trappings of self and explorations of life. I do not claim any authority over what I am sharing. It may be arrogant to assume that in a complex world of over seven billion people any one of us has an original thought. A thought that has not been shared and ruminated upon in the minds of thousands, millions, or even broadcasted collectively through the invisible threads that link us all. My aim is however, to give a voice of camaraderie to anyone who shares this curious path of understanding life and the human condition.

EVERY EXPERIENCE OFFERS US AN OPPORTUNITY TO LEARN.

My background is in Eastern Medicine. I have a bachelor's degree from the University of Central Florida. I studied broadcast journalism and humanities with an emphasis on philosophy. Shortly after college, I found myself in China teaching English. I landed in a foreign country peppered with new and exciting foods, languages, traditions, and religions. It was though the snow globe I lived habitually within for the first twenty years of my life was instantly shaken. The flakes fell in new places and in ways that made me suddenly aware of the permeability of our brains and the way we view the world. With conventional school behind me, I became keenly aware that I was entering a new classroom. It was a classroom Oprah would refer to as the school of life. Every experience offers us opportunities to learn. On the docket first, was an introduction to both yoga and Buddhism. To be fair, I was more or less dragged to my first yoga class. I was teaching at an English college in Yangshuo, rural China. This small city by Chinese standards inhabited just 250,000 people. It's the home to Karst mountains, the Yi river, and the highest concentration of English colleges in all of China. Most of my students were my age or older. The students knew basic English and had established careers. They enrolled in English college to improve their oral skills in hopes of gaining international opportunities and promotions in their respective fields. During the summer months, the college would be flooded with students and English teachers from all over the world; primarily Australia, England, and the Philippines. But I arrived to China in January. The campus was quiet and there were only four or five other international teachers there at the time. So, in a new environment, knowing no one, having already read all the books I brought with me, and unable to even watch television because I didn't understand Mandarin; I found myself feeling lonely. Sophie, one of the girls on the administration team at the school invited me to a yoga class. Solicited as a remedy for feeling lonely, I entered a small room that was stuffed to the brim with thirty or forty Chinese women of all ages. Packed in like sardines, the women looked like graceful porcelain statues as they held various poses. Everyone 18 to 80 years old folded in half and plopped like pancakes onto the studio floor. The suppleness of these human bodies was astounding. I recall thinking, "Wow, I wonder if the way they eat and perhaps even think contributes to their flexibility? I can't imagine a room full of Americans, especially in their eighties, being quite so limber. I want to know their secrets." Around this same time, I befriended Missy, my new roommate from the Philippines. Missy began accompanying me to yoga. She opened my eyes to Buddhism by lending me her book, *The Art of Happiness* by the 14th Dalai Lama. After I finished the book, I read another and another. Yoga for me was a game of show and tell. My Mandarin was pretty much nonexistent. The teacher's english was remedial. During the long narratives in Shavasana, which is the final resting portion of a yoga class, I assumed the teacher was guiding us through a meditation. I couldn't follow it so I inserted some of the meditations I was learning from the books on Buddhism. As I draped my sweaty body over the yoga mat, I rested in the dark and silently repeated the Buddhist prayer, "Inhale I breathe in; I calm my body. Exhale I breathe out; I calm my mind. Inhale, I breathe in the present moment. Exhale, I acknowledge what a wonderful moment it is." I floated on the sea of peace the words provided me. In retrospect, I suppose I created kind of a hybrid buddhist-yogic experience for myself. I had no clue what I was doing, but I knew I was feeling—feeling differently; better even. This was my first insight that there was much to discover and I was indeed discovering.

My time in China parlayed into my first adventure to India. Towards the end of my first year in China, my yoga teacher pulled me aside to acknowledge my dedication to the practice of yoga. She recognized my passion and recommended I go to India to study. One balmy night she sat with me at a picnic table. In her broken English, she told me about where she studied in Rishikesh in Northern India. She wrote down the name of the city and school on a tiny piece of wrinkled paper. I took note. My compulsion to go to India was too strong to ignore. I went home to the U.S. for the holidays. After catching up with family and friends, I flew back to Asia. My initial goal was to take a six week yoga course. The course would certify me to teach yoga, which at the time, teaching didn't interest me. I just wanted to immerse myself in the culture and attach language to this new activity that had quickly become my favorite pastime. At that point, I had never done yoga with english instruction. I was eager to see what could be revealed.

Six weeks in India turned into six months. I came to understand that yoga is not just an activity or hobby, it is a philosophy. An elaborate school of thought that dates back thousands of years. My mind was blown. Yet again, my snow globe was shaken. Turned upside down, the framework of my life was scrambled once again. I learned about the eight limb yogic path, meditation, Hinduism, and mythical Gods. I attended Kumbh Mela, the largest religious festival in the world. Millions of people gathered to bathe in the cleansing powers of the holy Ganges river. They do this during a reportedly auspicious time. My senses were overwhelmed by the wafting scent of incense and ambrosial spices, blended with the excrement from the millions of people who set up tents to camp in the open fields near the river. The stench molded with the smell of cows and hogs rolling in small mountains of garbage. My young eyes didn't know what to make of it all. My mind couldn't keep up with everything my eyes devoured. I remember the moment in the middle of the chaotic scene, I closed my eyes, took a deep breath, and said, "Be here now. Remember this moment." I didn't know much, but I knew I was being molded. On the level of spirit, I recognized that experience was reshaping my life as I knew it.

My inaugural experience in India was largely euphoric and profound, but it was also challenging. The relentless heat, the flies, cultural dissonance, and eventual longing to see my family wore me down over time. On one of my last days, I was in Agra, home of the Taj Mahal. The forecast said, "115 degrees and blowing dust." The environment felt unbearable, and I was one of the lucky ones. I wasn't homeless in desolate conditions. I wasn't begging for money wondering how I'd feed my family. All my basic needs were met, and while this might normally go unmentioned, my time in India made me grateful for things I previously took for granted. In many parts of the world, clean water is a luxury. My five dollar a night budget hotel room even had an old air conditioning units that fit into the window sill and blew subpar air that could be considered cool if you stretched your imagination. I wasn't dying, but I was very uncomfortable. I lost 20 pounds and my hunger for a reverse cultural immersion clicked in. I was ready to go home. Long story short, a few days later, I made it back to America.

I settled back into Western life—plush towels, air conditioning, and meals that were no longer shared with swarms of flies. Home felt nice. Very nice. Counter to my initial intention, I did indeed wind up teaching yoga. A couple years into teaching I was craving another mouthful of culture and dose of deeper knowledge. I returned to India.

OUR MINDS AND BODIES ARE NOT TWO SEPARATE ENTITIES, BUT RATHER, THEY ARE INTRINSICALLY CONNECTED.

This time I visited Kerala in the south of India and was introduced to Ayurveda. Ayurveda is the oldest form of holistic medicine. This form of medicine is premised on the concept that we are all made up of some permutation of five elements: ether, air, fire, water, and earth. The five elements in their unique proportions, comprise our mind-body constitutions, or what Ayurveda refers to as doshas. The core concept is that our minds and bodies are not two separate entities, but rather, they are intrinsically connected. In other words, the way we think affects the mechanisms within the body. The functions of the body influence the way we think and feel. According to Ayurveda and yogic principles, all disease originates in the mind. Insert mind-blown emoji here. The contents of this book are about placing the contents of our minds under a compassionate microscope. The intention is to dismantle fear in efforts to lead the most fulfilling life possible.

CHAPTER TWO

Fear is the Disease
Love is the Cure

UPON INTRODUCTION TO Ayurveda, I had what I describe in my first book, Your Life is Medicine: Ayurveda for Yogis, a serendipitous experience. I was fast asleep in bed one night. At 3:00 a.m. I heard a voice, yes, literally a voice in my bedroom say, "You must study Ayurveda." I instantly popped out of bed and dashed to my computer to research Ayurveda schools. The following year I graduated from the Kriplau School of Ayurveda in Massachusetts. I now spend a good portion of my life counseling clients on how to use Eastern Medicine and yogic principles such as balanced nutrition, meditation, and herbs to prevent disease and heal the mind and body naturally. Teaching people how to understand the mind-body connection and how to align with the internal intelligence that resides within each of us has become my career.

FEAR IS THE NUCLEUS OF OUR INDIVIDUAL AND SHARED SUFFERING.

The nature of this work is therapy-based and deeply personal. Over the years, I have had the privilege of engaging with thousands of clients and students. We dive deep to try to uncover the root of what ails us and the heights of what inspires us. As we courageously inquire into what causes disease in the mind-body, the core cause seems consistent. Fear.

Fear is the cause of disease. Holistic medicine holds true that disease is the disconnect from ease. Fear has an impeccable way of breaking the flow of ease that should flood the natural currents of life. Fear is at the nucleus of our individual and shared suffering. There is healthy fear. Healthy fear is the jumpy feeling that accompanies heights and loud noises. Sensible fear indicates if someone or something is friend or foe. That kind of fear has helped our species survive since that dawn of man. That is not the kind of fear I'm referring to. The type of fear I'm talking about here is a purposeless fear that generates anxiety, self-doubt, isolation, self-sabotage, and other undesirable experiences on the continuum of possible experiences. Like you, I know these feelings all too well. I've been aware of a looming sense of fear for as long as I can remember. A fear of being rejected, shamed, abandoned, and disappointed. Apart from these feelings I've also known their opposites—acceptance, confidence, connection, and satisfaction. It seems to be that goodness can prevail even in the presence of fear.

Fear holds us back in incredulous ways. Established in my hypothesis that fear is the main hindrance to happiness, in addition to being the cause of needless suffering, I have become nearly obsessed with understanding the origin and survival mechanisms of fear. I want to learn where fear came from and how to strip it of its power. My dream is to abolish fear and sit soundly in deep inner peace. This is my hope for myself and every other being on earth.

Right out of the gate, I'm noting on the record, I don't have all the answers. What I do have is a portfolio of inquiries, experiential data, revelations, and noteworthy teachings gathered from Eastern traditions, schools of psychology, and spirituality. This book is about vanquishing fear and amplifying love. I have no qualms in admitting I am a self-help junkie. My book shelves are stuffed with an embarrassing amount of literature on these themes. I have spent the better part of my adult life collecting data and pearls of wisdom that have shaped my life. I'm writing this book because I have a visceral and maybe overly enthusiastic reverence for books. The way I see it is, if someone spent a hefty portion of their life examining and crafting a portfolio of knowledge that we can extract life-changing inspiration and tools from in a matter of hours, why would we not leap at this opportunity? I'm bursting at the seams with a bubbling energy, pools of knowledge, and practical tools to ameliorate our lives by silencing the ways fear screeches through our souls. I'll blend Eastern traditions, western thought leaders, books such as *A*

Course in Miracles, The Yoga Sutras, The Four Agreements, and others to help you fall in love with yourself, your life, and the world around you.

Moving forward, each chapter will include: a Story, a Truth, and a Practice. The Story is my personal narrative. The Truth is an explanation of the theme based on a philosophical, religious, or scientific perspective. And the Practices are comprised of practical and spiritual tools that can be integrated into your life. This book is for anyone who is seeking love and intimacy in their lives. This book is for anyone who wrestles with the many faces of fear including anxiety, depression, self-sabotage, relentless business, and insecurity. This book has been crafted to help us navigate our relationship with Self and the relationship with others with a deeper level of understanding, grace, and fortitude. This book is not for the frightened sceptic. The concepts in this book rise above the typical Western mindset of "Keeping up with the Jones" and "Living the American Dream" which have been by in large manipulated by fear. The love in your heart is bigger than that. To truly unshackle ourselves from the bondage of fear and come to unambiguously know love, we need to face the misperceptions that frighten us the most.

If you've ever partaken in a deep clean of your closet, you know things can get messy before they look pristine. This process will require us to unpack old beliefs that have been stowed away for too long. This book will scare the bejesus out of fear, so please don't place it down when you get uncomfortable. Under fear there is love. Stay with this. Keep reading, and throughout your sacred and beautiful journey, stay the course.

Let's begin from a place of ease and relaxation. We must know that we are exactly where we're meant to be. We are here for a reason. We are safe and protected in this journey of understanding and healing. We have a shared intention of loving and being loved in return. Darling, the time has come; it's time to find your fearless heart.

My motive was romance.

To be fair, my main motivation for conquering the voice of self-hate, eradicating fear, and learning to love myself was actually incentivized by my desire to not just fall in love, but come to a place in my life where I could attract and sustain an elevated romantic relationship. I knew that despite my yearning to be in a state of love with a wonderful person, the type of love I dreamed of would be inconceivable if the voice of fear and self-hate continued to take residency in my head and steer the trajectory of my life.

I've always been in love with the idea of love. Early in my twenties, thrown into a casual conversation, a woman said, "I am my own soul mate." I recall feeling disenchanted, yet intrigued. When it came to love stories I had prescribed to what I had been taught by romantic comedies and Disney movies. Love is accompanied by fancy dresses, nice suits, and magic carpet rides. The prospect of being your own soul mate didn't match the archetypes that had been displayed before me. And as it turns out, those fantastical archetypes I consumed as a child were perilous stories indeed. They taught my mind to seek fulfillment in illusions over truth. Yuval Noah Harari, historian and author writes, "Romantic Comedies are to love as porn is to sex, and Rambo is to war. And if you think you can press some delete button and wipe all traces of Hollywood from your subconscious and your limbic system, you are deluding yourself." As I ponder on these concepts and sit to write this book, I'm realizing the concepts in this book were not examined to satisfy ephemeral love with a partner. To say relationships can be tricky is an understatement. Relationships, especially the ones that are worthwhile, reveal more to us about ourselves than often times comfortable to know. Relationships can be challenging, if not grueling at times. But on the other side of that coin, they are enlightening and joyous endeavors as well. It seems there is no discount on love. There is no shortcut or panacea we can quickly take to make relationships as easy as they are gratifying. It seems explicit. To love another person well, to make a relationship authentically fulfilling—we must first love ourselves with extraordinary courage and commitment. This book at its core is about learning to love the self.

I realized I have to become my own soul mate to engage with other soul mates. Once self-love is mastered, any love is possible. My disenchantment with the concept of being your own soul mate stemmed from a preconceived notion that being my own soul mate would be isolating.

THAT'S WHY HEARTBREAK IS SO SHATTERING. IT'S NOT ONLY THAT WE'RE LOSING SOMEONE WE CARE ABOUT; IT'S THAT WE'RE TRAPPED IN A ROOM WITH THE VOID OF LOVE WE'RE MISSING THE MOST. OUR OWN.

But being your own soul mate is not a lonesome endeavor. The exact opposite is true. I've come to learn that not loving myself is rock bottom loneliness. If I don't love myself it doesn't matter what love I receive. It'll be transient, and as it ebbs and flows or when it's gone, I'll be alone. And if I don't love myself, being alone is crushing. That's why heartbreak is so shattering. It's not only that we're losing someone we care about; it's that we're trapped in a room with the void of the love we're missing the most. Our own. Falling in love with ourselves not only makes being alone sweeter; it softens the fear around falling in love with someone else. Once we have our own love, the fear of ever being alone vanishes. Loving ourselves makes loving other people easier and more probable.

As the adage goes, *We see the world not as it is, but as we are.* The world we see is a reflective hologram of our own minds. We're constantly projecting. If we see ourselves as unloveable and fundamental flawed with never ending reasons to condemn our very being, we find ways to validate our belief that we are unloveable. We build walls to keep our vulnerabilities safe. Furthermore, we see other people as being equally unloveable and flawed and collect reasons to push them away. That is isolation. Love, specifically self-love, is non-discriminatory and inclusive. Loving ourselves abundantly translates into having abundant love towards everyone else as well.

The mental prison and how to escape.

I've come to realize that for most of my life my ability to love myself was based on erroneous conditions and expectations I created for myself. I could only love myself if I looked, acted, performed, and lived a certain way that measured up to my own standards. If I fell short, the fickle love vanished. The odds of me living up to these porous conditions were impractical. I always fell short and put myself in a mental prison. A mental prison is a mindset of fear. Fear translated as lovelessness towards myself. So each morning I woke up with a need to earn my own love as a way to unleash from cuffs of fear that I practically strapped on myself. I put myself in a prison of sorts. What the hell? Then as though I was some sort of masochist, once self-love was momentarily attained through whatever self-improvement obstacle course I decided would be sufficient, I spent the rest of the day trying to keep the self-love I had "earned." It was nuts and exhausting! Here's a ridiculous but true example. When I wake up in the morning I have to exercise for hours before I can relax enough to let myself enjoy breakfast and officially start my day. If I don't exercise, I feel anxious (fearful) all day. F-ing craziness. Self-love shouldn't be something one has to earn. It should be inherent. The objective here is to renounce the belief that self-love needs to be earned. We, and yes, I'm still talking to myself here, need to hold true that we are enough as we are. It is our birthright to be loved, most importantly, by our own-selves.

Romantic partners reveal to us our ghosts and our goodness.

Love should be and can be abundant. The opposite of course, is scarcity. Fear is a mindset of scarcity, and the mindset of scarcity is tiresome. I fatigued so many relationships because I placed the same expectations and conditions I prescribed for myself onto others.

THE REALIZATION THAT WE ARE LOVE, ALLOWS US TO THINK, ACT, AND BE LOVING FORCES IN THE WORLD.

I sabotaged relationships because I projected my own insecurities onto my partners. I foolishly expected men to navigate through a trapeze of expectations, that could by the way, changed on a whim. I expected people to excel in my fear-based circus in order for me to feel happy enough with myself to love them. Ironically, knowingly or unknowingly, due to their own lack of self-love, they were likely doing the same thing to me. I've come to believe that where there is a lack of self-love there is a perilous three-ring circus built on expectations, changing conditions, and no real curriculum to win. It's a losing paradigm.

This is clearly not a book about attaining our perfect romantic partner, even though, full disclosure: that was basically my original intent. These concepts give us access and aid towards tackling the ultimate work of our life which is deeper and more global than even something I hold in high regard: romantic love. Finding the perfect romantic partner must be a symptom of the real work: the attainment of self-love. You may be thinking, *how is self-love global?* It seems explicit in self-love is Self, which is far more micro than macro. Good point, but remember that we see the world as we see ourselves. If we see ourselves as expressions of love, then we see the world as an extension of love. The realization that we are love allows us to think, act, and be loving forces in the world. We become manic generators of love and magnetic forces for love. When we love ourselves love becomes ubiquitous. This perspective and way of being benefits the world. Self-love is a love that has been liberated by cumbersome conditions and stipulations.

THE THINGS THAT AIL US
ARE BORN OF FEAR.

Self-love does not exist because of something one has done in the past or will do in the future. This is a love not based on what one has accomplished or contributed. This is a love that exists purely because one exists. Self-love fosters a relationship with one's self that absolves anxiety, depression, insecurity, and fears of any kind. The things that ail us are born of fear. Self-love is a gateway to a new level of happiness. A happiness that is untethered to one's appearance, assets, bank account, reputation, or any other temporary circumstance.

And yes, all circumstances are temporary. This type of happiness remains intact even if one is stripped of ideal circumstantial dressings.

The self-love I speak of reveals happiness in the nude—innocent and unencumbered. You can't love someone until you love yourself. It's sensible. The very phrase has an emotional cadence that's easily tossed around. Dear God, I've heard this phrase five *thousand times. But here's the kicker…I just got it!* I had what one would call an epiphany.

THE SELF-LOVE I SPEAK OF
REVEALS HAPPINESS IN THE NUDE;
INNOCENT AND UNENCUMBERED.

While this concept of self-love has been in incubation for decades now, my revelation came simply and suddenly. Generally when I put a large amount of energy and effort into something it is successful. I co-conspire with the universe well. I pray. I roll up my sleeves. I'm not bashful about heavy lifting. If I care about something, I'll make it happen. So here I am at 33 years old. So many areas of my life feel satisfying and fulfilling. I am fortunate to have a passionate career, good friends, and a loving family. The general components of a happy life are in place. But even in the midst of a myriad of positive elements, there was still this one missing piece I couldn't seem to get into alignment…my romantic relationships. (Believe me, my greatest wish was that 'relationships' need not be written as plural. That was the issue.) I had many fleeting relationships, but I desired a single lasting one. So as the story goes, I was coming off the tails of sequential two to three year relationships. I've been a serial monogamous since puberty. Failed relationships yes, but not necessarily failed because I learned something through each of them. As consistent with most young love—it's about data collection. I was figuring out what I wanted and what I didn't want. Early on, I chose men to rowel my parents, get attention, and build up my self-esteem; only then to desecrate my self-esteem.

I gave men and outside forces the power to decide for me how I would feel about myself. I continuously sought love through love outside of myself. Even when I chose people who could have been harmonious matches, I found flaws in them. I found reasons to criticize, sabotage, and ultimately leave. I thought I wanted to get married, have babies, and live the cinematic dream. I thought I wanted in my heart, so fervently, to be in love. What I didn't realize is that I spent a decade trying to be in love with the wrong person. The person I was meant to be in love with first, was me.

Let's be clear, loving yourself does not mean being a narcissist. Someone who loves themself is not arrogant or self-absorbed. A person who loves themself is just the opposite. A person who loves themself is one hundred percent unabashedly humble. Once we love ourself, we have nothing to prove to anyone; not even ourselves. This love is not based on what we project into the world. It wears zero facades. A person who loves themself in this way is not preoccupied with the way they are perceived. Judgements and condemnation dribble off the backs of this kind of self-love. When one is adorned in self-love, fear is unable to be absorbed.

In a state of self-love, the skin of truth is so thick the lies of fear can not seep in.

WHAT I DIDN'T REALIZE WAS THAT
I SPENT DECADES TRYING TO BE IN
LOVE WITH THE WRONG PERSON.
THE PERSON I WAS SUPPOSED TO
BE IN LOVE WITH FIRST, WAS ME.

CHAPTER THREE

Love is my Religion

Story:

BOB MARLEY NAILED it. *Love is my religion.* My parents were raised in religious households. My dad attended Catholic school. My mom's mom, Grananny, as we called her, was the bible school teacher at her Nazarene church. She took religion very seriously. As a kid, I attended Lutheran services every other Sunday with my dad, and Nazarene services once a month when we visited Grananny. I couldn't tell the difference other than my Grandmother passed Tic Tacs down the pews to keep the kids quiet and somewhat attentive.

LOVE IS THE GOAL OF ALL RELIGIONS. I THINK IF THE MAIN FIGURE HEADS OF ALL THE WORLDS RELIGIONS WERE TO GATHER AT A ROUND TABLE AND DISCUSS THE AIM OF RELIGION JESUS, ALLAH, BUDDHA, MOSES, SHIVA, KRISHNA, AND THE OTHERS WOULD ALL BE ON THE SAME PAGE. LOVE IS A THE BACKBONE OF GOD.

I wasn't overly interested in church or God for that matter. I did however enjoy getting dressed up, spending time with my family, and hopefully going out to eat, or enjoying Grananny's amazing cooking after the service. In middle school, a few of my close friends were involved and excited about youth ministries. This for me translated into fun summer church camps, after school bible studies centered around homemade cookies sprinkled with a little talk of scriptures, and songs that I found uplifting and positive. Church, religion, and God took on a semblance of fellowship.

I developed a more intimate relationship with God when I was 15 years old. I began to pray. In a proverbial state of confusion and fear that might very well be a standard accompaniment to being a teenager, I needed God. I didn't have a name or face to go with this God, but I had a feeling. I had a feeling that there was someone or something that had my, had our, best interest at heart. I talked to this God. As I've gained exposure to various cultures and religions from all over the world, I still hold a conviction that love is the goal of all religions. I think if the main figure heads of all the world's religions were to gather at a round table and discuss the aim of religion, they would all be on the same page. I believe Jesus, Allah, Buddha, Moses, Shiva, and Krishna would all point to a common denominator: love. Love is a the backbone of God. Religious wars and fear-based doctrines are not God; not the God I know. When I speak about God in this book, I'm referring to the God of your understanding. You can call this God Love. Call it what you will. If you don't have an idea of God in your heart, perhaps look deeper into the traits of that fictitious name you shout when faced with "oh shit" moments. There's a pulsation within and around you that is silently guiding and supporting you. That's God.

Truth:

Let's take a look at what various religions have to say about love. Buddhism is referred to as the path of freedom and the religion of love. While Buddhism is more of a philosophy than a religion, the Buddha is viewed as a God-like figure. Buddhism teaches us that love that clinging, lust, confusion, neediness, fear, or grasping is not love, but is actually bondage or a limitation. Buddhist author Thich Nhat Hanh writes, "Understanding is another name for love. Loving others is understanding their suffering." In Catholicism, the famous scripture so often used at weddings, Corinthians 13:13 says, "Faith, Hope, and Love, and the greatest is Love." The Catholic churches places emphasis on love for God. The Bible states, "The theological virtue by which we love God is above all things for his own sake, and our neighbor as ourselves for the love of God." In Hinduism, love is referred to as Kama, or the feeling that "sends desire quivering into our heart." Similar to Catholicism, the highest love is a love for God; referred to as Bhakti, or devotion to God.

IN TAOIST TEACHINGS, LOVE IS REFERRED TO AS "SELF-NURTURING", OR LOVING ONESELF AND ESTABLISHING SELF-WORTH. THE TAO READS, 'CAN YOU NURTURE YOUR OWN SPIRIT WHILST HOLDING ONTO ONENESS?'...

In Islam traditions, it is stated that love has to be enlightened. The texts state, "Sacred love is the love that is realistic and enlightened." It is believed that one should not let one's feeling for something or some person make him neglect the whole truth. In alignment with Catholicism and Hinduism, love for God is above all other forms of love.

In Jainism, love is defined as non-violence, sociability, compassion, and a peaceful coexistence. Love is unity. Jainism delineates love into three categories: 1. Love of body, 2. Love of material objects, and 3. Love of past actions and consciousness. In this tradition, love is a blend of happiness and suffering. In the Jewish faith, it is said, "Love thy neighbor as thyself." According to the Jewish school of thought, kindness is central to loving. "Mitzvah" is informally known as good deed or an offering of kindness. This is an expression of love.

In Taoist teachings, love is referred to as "self-nurturing" or loving oneself and establishing self-worth. The Tao reads, "Can you nurture your own spirit whilst holding onto oneness? Can you connect with the Qi (energy) of your sensitivity, creating imagination, and determination whilst harmonizing with We Wei (dynasty)? Can you understand your human centered mind without corrupting your Tao-mind? And can you do this all whilst loving and nourishing yourself rather than indulging in self-interest and selfishness? Then can you truly love all people without harming yourself, allowing others to rise to their fullest whilst not diminishing your own stature?" And finally, John 4:18 says, "There is no fear in love. But perfect love drives out fear. Because fear has to do with punishment. The one who fears is not made in perfect love."

Practice:

While in India, I participated in a meditation activity where eight or so of us lined up in two rows. Each person sat directly across from another person. We were asked to stare into each other's eyes for several minutes (time flew, but it was probably about five minutes per person). We were requested to think silently, "The divine is within me. The divine is within you. I see the divine in me and in you." We then changed partners and repeated the exercise and until we have sat across and gazed into the eyes of everyone in the room. By the end of the meditation, we were asked if we were able to experience the divine within ourselves and each other.

It could have been easy for me to carry skepticism and reservations towards this activity. I could have written it off as hokey. But I'm glad I didn't because I would have missed out on the phenomenal experience of losing my attachment and identification to this physical sense of self and inherent separation from others that accompanies identifying as a separate human. I really did experience myself as a vehicle for the divine and saw the other women as vessels of divinity as well. During the exercise and the weeks that followed, these women and I continued to study and live together at the ashram. To me, these women looked like angelic beings. The practice of intentionally choosing to see myself and others as divine creatures transmuted my habitual and analytical observations into a more heavenly or love-centric perspective. You can try this. Grab a friend or family member and sit across from them. Make your space and physical body as comfortable as possible. Gaze deeply into their eyes and repeat to yourself silently, "The divine is within me. The divine is within you. I see the divine in me and in you." Notice the feelings you experience after the practice.

CHAPTER FOUR

The Role of Stories & Teachers

Story:

WHAT IF EARTH is just a huge classroom? What if we're cosmic creatures who have been called to report as human beings to the school of life for as long as it takes for us to learn our God-given lessons; lessons that promote self-awareness, growth, and evolution? I'm pretty sure that's what we're all doing here...just learning. With that being said, what if we soften our reactions towards the lessons at hand? What if we become more patient with ourselves as students? Parents and teachers are patient with their children and kids in the classroom. They know that fumbling and floundering is par for the course in the process of learning. Why have we as adults set the expectation that we should not be afforded the same amount of grace and patience that we extend to children? Why is being instantly astute at resolving the challenges before us an expectation that seems to just click on in adulthood? What if we were to see everyone in our lives as teachers? What if every experience was received as a learning activity? Our travels are cultural field trips, our relationships are subjects of interpersonal communications and conflict resolution, friday night happy hours are recess, and crisis are our big exams. While we're all given individual assignments and personal curriculums, the lessons are basically universal. The ultimate lesson being, *can we learn to love?*

WHAT IF WE SEE EVERYONE IN
OUR LIVES AS TEACHERS?

I've pondered over this concept many times and why it might sound fantastical, to me it feels realistic. I believe every sensation, experience, person, and thought reigns as a teacher. Once a lesson is learned we move on to a new or deeper aspect of that sensation, experience, person, or thought. Reiterating a story feels to me like staying in a classroom long after the lesson has been learned. Stories only seem relevant to revisit if the moral would be best shared through its telling. So yes, I like to share stories, but let me be clear; we are not our stories. Our stories can not be but colored by our own perspectives, lapses in memory, and the passage of time that happens in between the event and the telling of the event.

My mom loves telling a story about me as a toddler. As the story goes, my parents were hosting a family picnic for the entire extended family; aunts, uncles, cousins, and grandparents. Everyone was there. Recently potty-trained, I apparently had a fetish for my ruffled underwear. My mother says I decided to go into my bedroom and retrieve all twenty or so pairs of my assorted ruffled panties. I then meticulously lined up the panties, making a parade or trail of my tiny undergarments that traced from my bedroom, through the living room, through the back patio, and all the way out to the picnic tables in the backyard. I then took my aunt's hand and led her down my little path of panties pronouncing the color of each pair for her viewing and learning enjoyment. I find this story adorable and ridiculous. Was my mom's recount of this story accurate and factual? Probably not. The story has likely been embellished a fair bit. A friend of mine often says, "I never let a smudgy fact ruin a good story." You see, stories are just that, they're recollections. We can gain morals and lessons from stories, but let's not tie ourselves strictly to the tales we've been reciting on repeat. And in case you're wondering, I don't think there's any grand moral to my mom's favorite childhood story of me, other than I enjoyed colors, crafting shows, and sharing. This much I can siphon out to be true.

Truth:

A Course in Miracles is a book about transforming fear into love. It is essentially a psychological mind training manual. Divided into three sections: the text, the workbook, and the teacher's manual. The dense text teaches us how to see the world from the vantage point of love.

A COURSE IN MIRACLES SAYS, "IT'S NOT UP TO YOU WHAT YOU LEARN: IT'S MERELY WHETHER YOU LEARN THROUGH JOY OR PAIN."

To paraphrase from *A Course in Miracles*, every situation and experience, each person standing in front of you exists for your spiritual development. The only reason the situation is occurring in the first place is to serve as an assignment for you. With each assignment we are encouraged to apply our spiritual principles so that we can be better people day by day. But if you don't show up for the assignment and you let the ego and lack of awareness call the shots, the lesson has to reoccur again and again until you get it. If we don't recognize the person before us as a teacher, the same lesson will just arrive again through another person until we realize that's our teacher. That's our lesson. That's our unavoidable opportunity to learn. *A Course in Miracles* says, "It's not up to you what you learn: it's merely whether you learn through joy or pain." The faster we recognize the role of the teacher and the meaning within the experience, the more painless and perhaps even enjoyable the assignment. When we become able-bodied learners we become what The Course calls, Happy Learners

Practice:

In order to be stellar students we need to be willing to learn. When a person or situation appears ask yourself, What is this here to teach me? Go inside and listen with a willingness to hear the answer. Open your eyes and ears to the person and environment at hand. Really see. Really listen. What comes up for you may feel uncomfortable. It may reveal to you that you are invited to release selfishness, jealousy, attachment to beauty, or whatever it may be. To be concrete—access a situation that is occurring in your life right now. Grab a piece of paper and write it down. For example, the guy I'm dating is being distant and I am feeling insecure and jealous.

Write down this question, What is this here to teach me? Sit. Breathe. Jot down possible responses. For example, This assignment is here to teach me to release jealousy. This assignment is here to teach me to trust another person. This assignment is here to teach me to trust my intuition and this gut feeling that something is off with him. This assignment is here to teach me that my jealousy about this man potentially leaving me for another woman is not about the man or another woman, but about me. It's about my fear of being abandoned or whatever it may be. Just write it down. We do not have to obtain answers instantly. Remember, we are children that are still learning. We can be afforded the same level of patience we afford to kids. The answer will surface in due time. Bertrand Russell writes, "It's not the answer that enlightens us, but the question"...The questions is, What is this here to teach me? The opportunity to learn joyfully is upon us.

CHAPTER FIVE

See the World not as It is, but as We are

Story:

IT WAS TWO years into my Ayurveda practice when I rented a little treatment room within a yoga studio. I poured my soul into my clinical practice. I was learning, doing my best to practice what I preach, and striving to grow my business. My efforts were paying off. On this particular day, I saw five clients back to back. For seven or eight hours, I sat across from women going over their current food intake, lifestyle habits, and daily rhythms.

Together, through the lens of natural medicine, we were excavated ways to improve their wellbeing. One of the first questions I ask when people sit down is, "What brings you in? Is there anything in particular you'd like to address today?" Each woman opened up and revealed the various imbalances they wished to remedy. These challenges ranged from arthritis, to digestive pain, to high cholesterol. As I sat there, intently listening to their every word and providing solutions based on this holistic science, I couldn't help but notice all of these women seemed anxious. Their faces looked calm and their voices were stable and attentive. But I felt strong waves of jitters emanating from their presence. I could feel their nervous systems were hyper and hurried. But the interesting part was none of these women mentioned anxiousness as a theme in their lives. After addressing the imbalances they were most aware of, I asked them if they felt anxious. They all took a long pause and said, "Hmmm, not really, but maybe a little." *Interesting,* I thought to myself. I'm picking up on anxiety, but it doesn't seem to be a real issue in my clients' lives.

That evening I joined my parents for dinner. My mom asked about my day. I told her it was great. I met amazing new clients. I felt helpful and fulfilled, and everyone seemed receptive and empowered. "But everyone seemed so anxious," I said. "Really? Is that why they were there?" my mom asked. "No, they all said anxiety wasn't an issue for them," I replied. My mom said, "Well, maybe you felt anxious then." Oh my gosh! Yes! That was it. As a new practitioner, I was used to only seeing two or three clients a day. That was my first day seeing five clients in a row. In the back of my mind throughout the day, I was keeping a close eye on the clock. Early on in my Ayurveda career consultations would sometimes run way over the allotted 75-90 minute session. I wanted to make sure I kept to my schedule on that day so that no one would be waiting in the lobby. I wanted to be respectful of my clients' time. However, my strict adherence to the clock was indeed making me a little anxious. I was just so zoomed into my clients that I didn't realize I was anxious. Being so focused on them made me think the anxiety was theirs. It was mine. We see the world not as it is, but as we are. This type of projection is happening all the time. Have you ever noticed how people who comprise their integrity by lying and cheating are the exact people who routinely think they're being lied to and cheated on.

WHO WE ARE, AND THE STATE OF OUR MIND IN ANY GIVEN MOMENT IS COLORING OUR EXPERIENCE, AND SHAPING THE WAY WE INTERPRET THE WORLD AROUND US.

Have you noticed how people with a loving nature think everyone in the world is kind? Have you ever noticed that when we're disheartened the color of the sky, trees, flowers, and even stop lights look less vivid. Conversely, when we're in love everything in the world looks so bright and happy! This is because who we are and the state of our mind in any given moment is coloring our experience and shaping the way we interpret the world around us.

Truth:

Steven Covey writes, "We see the world not as it is, but as we are—or how we are conditioned to see it. When we open our mouths to describe what we see, we are actually describing ourselves, our perceptions, our paradigms." Frank Brown said, "Many people have been wearing green glasses for so long, they think this really is an Emerald City."

IT'S LIKE THE WORLD IS A BLANK CANVAS AND WE'RE THE ARTIST. THE MASTERPIECE ISN'T ON THE CANVAS; NOT AT FIRST. IT'S IN OUR MINDS.

Henry David Thoreau wrote, "It's not what you look at that matters. It's what you see." And *A Course in Miracles* teaches us, "Perception is a mirror, not a fact." All of these thought leaders are mimicking the same concept. It is what is inside that creates what is outside. The world is not strictly black and white. Within the universe exists a continuum of everything you can possible fathom and more. The world is never just one way. We just happened to be viewing it that particular way based on our thoughts, our belief systems, and our choices.

If we are experiencing someone or something that is incongruent with our desires, we must first turn the lens inward and see what is going on inside of ourselves that is generating that projection. If we want to change our experience, we have to shift our inner landscape and choose to perceive the situation differently. Spiritual teacher and author, Wayne Dyer teaches us, "Change the way you look at things, and the things you look at change." It's a great big world out there. Whatever you want to see and experience exists. The question is, does it exist within you? It's like the world is a blank canvas and we're the artist. The masterpiece isn't on the canvas; not at first... It's in our minds.

So often I've been in relationships where I become swept up in the excitement of the novelty. A new person, new charms, attractive appearances, adoring remarks, and fun escapades. But then as time passed, what I initially perceived as novel faded into ordinary.

I NOW KNOW THAT WHEN MY AFFECTION FOR SOMEONE I ONCE FOUND INTOXICATING DIMINISHES, I NEED TO EXPLORE MY OWN HEART AND MY OWN MIND.

What I found captivating in the beginning changed shape into a picture of bemusement. I got bored and I left. I can see clearly now that the initial charm, attractiveness, adoration, and joy were real. It was real because I chose to create it. I chose to see the person in front of me as I chose to feel about myself. But as time went on, I became insecure about revealing my vulnerability, so I chose to see the person differently so that I had a reason to end the relationship. In most cases, the person didn't change. I changed. And when something changes from loving and positive to something far less positive, I know fear is responsible for the shift and it's my responsibility to adjust my inner state.

Now that I accept this empowering realization, I am more aware of how I see people. I now know that when a distinct thought about someone enters my mind, I need to go inward and inquire about myself. I now know that when my affection for someone I once found intoxicating diminishes, I need to explore my own heart and my own mind. I need to see if I am allowing my ego to change the way I'm viewing this person because fear has taken hold. And when I want to shift my perception to return to love, I know I have to shift from a fearful state to a state of love. This is not to say that we have to stay entangled with everyone we have ever loved. We can move in and out of one another's lives with grace and ease. There's a chance that when you perceive someone you were once entranced by as now being off putting, it could be because they indeed have changed. And their change was directed by what was going on within them. We're no different from each other. Just as your mind alters your perception and actions, everyone else's mind, perception, and actions are malleable as well. When one person shifts, we all shift. Love is not static. Relationships transform; that's not only natural, but necessary for our growth. But the shift should always be guided by awareness and an honest assessment, not by the corrosive functions of fear.

Practice:

Practicing gratitude is a wonderful way to shift from fear to love. Gratitude clears the debris that hinders our sightline towards seeing what is good, right, and divine.

GRATITUDE CLEARS THE DEBRIS
THAT HINDERS OUR SIGHTLINE
TOWARDS SEEING WHAT IS
GOOD, RIGHT, AND DIVINE.

If there's someone in your life in which you're undergoing a shift in perception towards; meaning, you used to see them as fabulous and now you see them as flawed; sit down and right a list of all their positive qualities. It may be difficult at first because your current perception of them is not shiny, but as you note their positive traits your mind will open up and you will become flooded with favorable and loving feelings towards them. When you put the pen down, you'll realize that only minutes have passed. That person did not change. You chose to see them differently. We can choose to see the world through eyes of love. When we love ourselves, loving others is automatic and habitual. When we lapse, we must go inside and reaffirm our own love.

CHAPTER SIX

The Small Self, the Big Self, & the Ego

Story:

I HAVE A horrible habit of looking at my phone out of boredom and impulse. Clearly, I live in the modern era, but in full disclosure I long for the days before social media. Like most people, at the dawn of social media, I used in sparingly. It was a fun little tool that brought me specs of joy as I randomly dabbled on the sites. But as the platforms grew and became more accessible on our smartphones, the omnipresent nature of the game crept into my life in alarmingly high portions. At one point, I caught myself checking my phone immediately upon rising, at stop lights, between clients, and dozens of times during the day, and again before bed. I was practically a technology/social media addict.

SOCIAL MEDIA IS GROSSLY EGO BASED. POLISHED PHOTOS AND CAPTIONS, METICULOUSLY CURATED STORIES, ALL BEAUTY, ALL "HAPPY", ALL A FACADE OF PERFECTION. SOCIAL MEDIA IS A GARISH STAGE FOR THE SELF. WE'VE ALL BECOME STARS IN OUR OWN REALITY SHOWS.

Here's the thing, while social media can be innocent and healthy enough if utilized with discipline and perspective, it is grossly ego-based. Polished photos and captions, meticulously curated stories, all beauty, all "happy," all a facade of perfection. Social media is a garish stage for the Self. The gremlin voice of inadequacy becomes louder as we peruse the highlight reel of other people's lives. We're seeing a full photograph, but we're not getting the whole picture. As we look at the glossy surface of someone else's life, we're comparing our insides with someone else's outside. It's apples to oranges, and it stings. We've all become stars in our own reality shows; only the show is not real. Even though many of us do our best to be authentic on social media, reality is simply far too nuanced and intimate to relay with any degree of accuracy. Social media can encourage self-inflating behaviors and can reinforce the ugliness that comes along with it.

One day I was walking on the beach and rather than enjoying the way the warm sun bounced off my skin or the way the water glistened or even the silky way the dolphins moved across the coastline, I was thinking about where I'd take my next photo and what I would write in the caption. Thank God, the grossness of my mindset caught my attention and forced me to reevaluate the way I was managing my time and energy. I decided to take social media off my phone, not because it's inherently bad or because I blatantly want to discourage other people from using it in healthy ways they see fit, but because it was distracting. I was allowing it to distort my Self and sense of Self. I was using social media to validate my Self. Upon taking the apps off my phone, I was able to break the habit of incessantly seeking fallacious external validation. A positive side effect was I felt more at ease; probably for a host of reasons, markedly being: I had more uninterrupted time with my Self.

Truth:

Historian Yuval Noah Harari states that our image of the self is based on stories, not reality. Our stories are myth makers. In 21 Lessons for the 21st Century, "In the age of Facebook and Instagram you can observe this myth making process more clearly than ever before, because some of it has been outsourced from the mind to the computer. It is fascinating and terrifying to behold people spending countless hours constructing and embellishing a perfect self online, becoming attached to their own creation, and mistaking it for the truth about themselves. That's how a family holiday fraught with traffic jams, petty squabbles, and tense silences becomes a collection of beautiful panoramas, perfect diners, and smiling faces; 99 percent of what we experience never becomes the story of the self. It is particularly noteworthy that our fantasy self tends to be very visual, whereas actual experiences are corporeal. In the fantasy you observe a scene in your mind's eye or on the computer screen. You see yourself standing on a tropical beach, the blue sky behind you, one hand holding a cocktail, the other arm around your lover's waist. Paradise.

AND JUST AS YOU ARE NOT THE WINDS, SO ALSO YOU ARE NOT THE JUMBLE OF THOUGHTS, EMOTIONS AND DESIRES YOU EXPERIENCE, YOU ARE CERTAINLY NOT THE SANITIZED STORY YOU TELL ABOUT THEM WITH HINDSIGHT.

What the picture does not show you is the annoying fly that bites your leg, the cramping in your stomach from eating the fish that had gone slightly off, the tension in your jaw from a big fake smile, and the ugly fight the happy couple had five minutes ago. If we could only feel what people in the photos felt while taking them! If you really want to understand yourself, you should identify less with your Facebook account or the inner story of the self. Instead, you should observe the actual flow of the mind and body. You will see your thoughts, emotions, and desires appear and disappear without much reason and without command from you, just as different winds blow from this or that direction and mess up your hair. And just as you are not the winds, so also you are not the jumble of thoughts, emotions and desires you experience, you are certainly not the sanitized story you tell about them with hindsight. You experience all of them. People ask, "Who am I?" and expect to be told a story. The first thing you need to know about yourself is that you are not a story."

There are levels to the concept of self. There are two ways to view the Self/self. The Self with the big (S), is the higher Self. The higher Self is connected to Source—God-like energy or the heart. The self with the lowercase (s), is the self that identifies with the ego or the mind. Self provides clarity, whereas self burdens us with confusion. Little (s) self operates at the level of the mind. The mind functions at the level of thought. Thoughts tend to be frenetic, analytical, and often gravely misinformed; whereas the Self in its purest state is aligned with truth and is far more trustworthy than the mind. Therefore, the Self is more desirable than the self. The Self has a macro perspective on life and the interconnectedness of all things, whereas the self has a more myopic view of life. The perspective of self is limited and self-serving. The self is ignorant and lacks the awareness to understand how everything functions together harmoniously. The Self is enlightened and realizes we are all connected in compelling and unfathomable ways.

What is the Ego?

The ego can have a bad reputation, but the ego is not always a bad thing. In its healthiest form, the ego is the aspect of self that gives form to our identity. It gives us reference to our place in the world. Its function is largely for orientation. For example, my ego teaches me to respond to my name, associate with my gender, and know where I'm from so I know what line to get into at customs while traveling. My ego helps me perform appropriately in relation to social cues. Ego hubris, or excessive self-importance is the troublemaker. You see, the ego is basically the mind. The mind is the unhinged generator of thoughts, some being of value and some meaningless. The slippery slope lies in becoming inordinately attached to our thoughts. When we become attached to our thoughts, we become attached to our identity. Once absorbed in the ego's making of our identity, we distance ourselves from our Self. For example, if I believe that my identity is being an author, and my identity strengthens based on people's opinions of my work, than my identity, or sense of self is precarious at best. If I am just my ego's interpretation of my identity, than who will I be when and if I no longer wish to write? Or who will I be if people don't praise my work? Will I be less than? Of course not. But if we believe that we are our thoughts, or scarier yet, the ego's idea of who we are in the world, than we risk losing connection to the Self.

Excessive reliance and dependence on the mind or ego can and will lead to egotism. Egotism leads to misery. It's a scandalous type of misery that seeps into our existence often without us even realizing it. We can too easily feel anxious and insecure without being able to put our finger on the reason. Egotism is the cause. It causes us to identify with the small self, at the expense of losing the Self. When this happens fear wins and in insidious ways such as feeling less than, overworking, and hinging our happiness on our successes—the Self suffers. The Self on the other hand surpasses worldly labels and markers of identity. The Self is not the CEO, mother, attorney, HR rep, nurse, etcetera. The Self is the soul animating as energy expressed through a human body at any given moment. Understanding that the ego is the mind working against us, actor Jim Carey shared this message in his commencement speech for Maharashi University in 2014. "The imagination is always manufacturing scenarios both good and bad and the ego will try to keep you trapped in the multiplex of the mind. Our eyes are not viewers, they are also projectors that are running a second picture that we see in front of us all the time. Fear is writing that script and the theme is, 'I'll never be good enough.' This is the voice of the ego. The ego will not let you rest until you've left an indelible mark on the earth, until you've achieved immortality. How tricky is this ego that it would tempt us with something we already possess?"

"AND THE MOMENT WE CEASE
TO IDENTIFY WITH THE EGO AND
BECOME AWARE THAT WE ARE THE
WHOLE ORGANISM, YOU REALIZE HOW
HARMONIOUS IT ALL IS, BECAUSE
YOUR ORGANISM IS A MIRACLE. ALL
OF THIS FUNCTIONING TOGETHER."

British philosopher Alan Watts offers insights on the topic of Self and ego. "To understand the self it doesn't need to remember anything. Just like you don't need to know how you work your thyroid gland. It just is…You don't know how to shine like the sun. You just do it. Like you breathe. Doesn't it astonish you that you are this fantastic complex thing that is doing all of this and you never received education in how to do it? You never learned this fortuitous miracle. From a strictly scientific perspective, this organism is a continuous energy with everything going on. If I am a foot; I am the sun. Only we have this little, partial view. I am something in this body. The ego. That's a joke. The ego is nothing other than the focus of conscious attention. It's like a radar. The radar on a ship is a troubleshooter. Is there anything in the way? And conscious attention is a design function of the brain to scan the environment like radar does and notes for any trouble making changes. And if you identify yourself with your troubleshooter then naturally you define yourself as being in a perpetual state of anxiety. And the moment we cease to identify with the ego and become aware that we are the whole organism, you realize how harmonious it all is, because your organism is a miracle. All of this functioning together. All the things functioning together; even the corpus pools that are fighting each other in your bloodstream and eating each other up; if they weren't doing that you wouldn't be healthy. So what is at discord at one level of your being is harmony at a higher level, and you begin to realize that and begin too to realize the discord of your life and the discord of peoples lives in which are a fight at one level of the universe are harmonious at a high level." Essentially, the ego is fear centric. When we operate from the unconscious level of self, we're ensnared in the proverbial trap of fear and littleness. Conversely, when we elevate to the level of Self, we exalt above the onerous reverberations of fear. At the level of self, we're partially blind to the lyrical designs of life. The self is so easily distracted by what's wrong or what could possibly go wrong, that it loses sight of all that is right. At the level of Self, we have a broader perspective, so we're not inundated and misguided by fear. The Self appreciates the bigger picture.

Practice:

I find the easiest place to seamlessly unclinch from the trappings of self and connect to Self is in nature. Nature is a living, breathing ecosystem of harmonious connection. The Sufi poet Hufiz writes, "Even after all this time the Sun never says to the Earth, you owe me. Look what happens with a love like that, It lights the whole sky." Nature is selfless. She knows nothing of the ego and the pain it causes. Nature is patient, generous, and attuned.

Free yourself from your gadgets and agenda. Take a few minutes, a few hours, or better yet, a few days to just go outside. Sit in the grass, feel your feet on the earth, watch the way clouds shift in the sky, feel how the temperature rises and falls without any regard for the number. Nature doesn't measure her steps or calculate her every move. She doesn't need to. When we align with the Self and universal intelligence that pure knowing supersedes, all ego constructs. Go outside and bask in nature's beauty. You'll drop the ego and feel the Self.

Dear Ego,

I wanted to write a song and celebrate releasing you, but you've told me for so long that I can not sing. But one day I'll belt out lyrics and God will burst through my throat and it'll sound glorious, as to say F-you ego. You don't know me. Ego, you don't know yourself. You're in a constant identity crisis; which is ironic because all you are is identity... the inconsequential small stuff: our names, our appearances, our cars, and clothes...littleness. Ego, I am so much bigger than you. I am spirit on an average day and soul on a great day. Every single day I am bigger than you. You invaded my mind when I was a child; before I knew of judgment and fear. You spotted my innocence and you robbed me. But ego, I've stolen my Self back. I've reclaimed justice and what was rightfully mine. For you borrowed my purity and goodness, but you didn't use it wisely. It didn't make you better. It made you bigger and greedier. God made me wiser, and redemption always has its time. So, I'm sorry ego, your time is done here. Goodbye to you and what you stand for: scarcity, comparison, inflated sense of self, perfectionism, and all that makes my soul gasp for air. I can breathe again.

CHAPTER SEVEN

Power of Thought

Story:

MY CHILDHOOD BEST friend and I used to sit around and dreamscape our lives. We'd envision being bridesmaids in each others weddings. We hadn't had our first real kiss yet, but we were already writing Maid of Honor speeches. With a strong imagination, and unadulterated ideals, I thought I knew exactly how my life would pan out. As a 10-year-old, 30 seemed old. So, I had it all sorted out. I decided very early on that I'd leap over benchmarks and have it all, all before I turned thirty.

My best friend Ashley and I sat there in cheerleading shorts rolled up around the waist. Our hair was pulled back in sloppy ponytails. We were giddy with certainty and seeded with a robust enthusiasm for our powers to create. Create that is, all according to our own well-meaning, and naive master plan. My plan was to fall in love in high school. I would marry the first man I fell in love with and gave my virginity to. We'd go away to university together. I'd study journalism and he'd study art, literature, or law. Something thought provoking and powerful. We'd get married shortly after graduation.

OUR THOUGHTS HOWEVER POSITIVE, CANNOT AND SHOULD NOT BE USED TO ATTEMPT TO CONTROL OR MICROMANAGE OUR LIFE STORY AND SOULS' PATH.

It'll be no surprise to you that we'd buy a house complete with a red front door and a white picket fence. Heck, we might as well throw in a golden retriever that would run around in the faultless green grass in the front yard. I'd establish a successful career as a TV news reporter and catapult up the career ladder to be a lead anchor by the age of 26. Why the hell not? By 27, I'd give birth to my first baby girl. We'd name her Lilly. And by 29, her brother would be born. I'd be 30 years old, madly in love with my high school sweetheart turned husband, and living in a sweet all-American home. I'd be a successful television personality and the mother of two adorable children. Oh, and Ashley and I would still be best friends. Ta-da! Isn't that how life works out? You think up a plan, you believe in your dream, you stay focused on it, and it transpires in the exact sequencing you so astutely designed. Not quite, and thank God for that. Granted, that could have been a magical life, if it was indeed the life intended for me. But it was not. And trying to force a life that is not in alignment with the universes' larger plan is not world's easiest way to achieve happiness.

We have complete power over our thoughts. It is our prerogative and soulful imperative to keep the quality of our thoughts at a high resonance. Positive thoughts should be the catalyst for our feelings, actions, and general response to life. But our thoughts, however positive, can not and should not be used to attempt to control and micromanage our life story and souls' path. You've probably pieced together by now that "the life of my dreams" I envisioned as a little girl is not the life I am living. I did fall in love in high school, but that boy happened to be a bit of a lost soul. Under his influence with the cooperation of my own poor decisions, I slipped down a path littered with drugs and a three year slurry of awful decisions. That relationship ended before college. At university, I did indeed study journalism, but during my senior year I interned at a news station and quickly realized I had no business being a reporter. I found the newsroom atmosphere to be competitive and the content of the news too depressing for my liking.

Instead of becoming a reporter upon graduation, I ended up backpacking through Europe. I met people from all over the world and learned that being an English teacher to non-english speaking students in foreign countries could be a intriguing experience. Instead of getting married and buying an all-American house with a statement red door, I told my on-and-off again college boyfriend goodbye and moved to China to teach English. Rather than catapulting up the career ladder, I found yoga. I moved to India. I found Ayurveda. I was nearing the age of 27 and I was opening my first Ayurveda clinic. I had no husband, no corporate job, and no adorable children. Yet, I was happy! Beyond happy. I was peaceful and fulfilled. See, life doesn't have to happen according to our "plan." Life will be peppered with surprises, change of direction, failures, comebacks, and unlimited opportunities to evolve. If I would have used my power of thought to adhere strictly to my childhood plan, I would have come up against resistance time and time again. I would have robbed myself of the happiness life was trying to offer me, all in the name of naivety and control. Thank God something inside of me reinforced time and time again that I should remain positive and open to the experiences presented to me. When I relinquished scrupulous authority over my plan, I learned and am still learning of a grander plan. My job isn't to think up a plan. My job is to keep the narrative in my head love centric, and the speech towards others kind. My job is to keep my thoughts in an elevated state as to align and support my life's journey.

Truth:

If experience has taught me anything, it's that our thoughts create our reality. Revered philosophers have pondered this concept for millennia. Psychologists have entrenched themselves in research to support this theory for the last 100 plus years, and the most renowned physicist of all time has proven this to be true. Maslow, Einstein, and Socrates all describe a direct correlation between one's reality and one's thoughts. If we want to be the fabulous co-creators of our life that we were born to be, we have to take care to tame and train the thinking mind. Everything both good and bad that we perceive in this life originates in the mind. Publishing mogul Louise Hay writes, "I don't fix my problems. I fix my thinking and the problem fixes itself." Spiritual teacher Sri Chinmoy teaches us, "Thinking is becoming, therefore be extremely careful in your thinking." Activist Mahatma Gandhi said, "A man is a product of his thoughts. What he thinks, he becomes." Psychologist Abraham Maslow said, "The ancestor to every experience is a thought." Author Lisa Hayes states, "Be careful how you are thinking of yourself. You are listening." Randi G. Fine wrote, "Our thoughts are very powerful. When we focus on what we lack we create blockages and limitations. We become imprisoned by the vibration of negative energy. As a result, we attract what we think, which in this case is negativity, while repelling the very things we desire." The wise sage, our very own Yoda from Star Wars enlightens us, "Fear is the path to the dark side. Fear leads to anger. Anger leads to hate. Hate leads to suffering." Fear is a concept implanted by the ego and immortalized only by the thoughts it leeches on to. Varied thought leaders from all over the world for thousands of years have been reiterating the same truth in different ways. And finally, Buddha said, "What we think, we become."

Loving thoughts emanate a positive and high vibration or high frequencies. Thoughts of fear emanate negative and low vibration or low frequencies. High frequencies generate a mood of being happy, peaceful, generous, forgiving, creative, imaginative, adaptable, and amicable. Low frequency thoughts create a downward spiral in tones of anger, depression, guilt, blame, resentment, regret, and malaise. Albert Einstein confirmed, "Everything is energy and that is all there is to it. Match the frequency of the reality you want and you can not help but get that reality. It can not be any other way. It is not philosophy. It is physics." Actress Erykah Badu said, "I think people who vibrate the same frequency, vibrate towards each other. They call it, in science, sympathetic vibrations."

"THE MOTION PICTURE OF YOUR LIFE WAS MADE MANIFEST BY THE DIRECTOR OF DIVINE CREATION IN PERFECT FORM BEFORE YOU GOT HERE. YOUR MOTION PICTURE IS SPECTACULAR BEYOND ANYTHING YOU OR I COULD EVER DREAM UP."

Dr. Masaru Emoto, a Japanese scientist, verified that our thoughts and feelings affect our physical reality. He conducted a scientific study by producing different focused intentions through written thoughts, spoken words, and music. He literally presented them to water samples. He cataloged how the water molecules changed their expression as an effect of the sentiments being offered to them. With a high-speed camera, he was able to photograph the way water molecules crystallized. He found that the water samples exposed to loving words crystallized into brilliant, complex, and colorful snowflake patterns. In contrast, water exposed to negative thoughts expressed as incomplete formations, asymmetrical patterns, and dull colors.

Thoughts certainly affect our reality and are very much a mechanism of control. Our thoughts play the role of the "director" of our lives. Imagine this, at the time of your creation, God created for you your own personal divine movie. Throughout the course of your life it was promised to you that you would be gifted everything necessary to create the movie of your dreams. You would be given main actors, supporting characters, extras, settings, set designers, lighting, wardrobe, multiple scripts, and everything else you needed to be the ultimate creator of this miraculous Oscar-worthy motion picture. Your only job in this production is to play the role of the director. You must use your thoughts to actively, yet positively, manipulate all of your personal movie-making elements to bring your movie to the big screen (to life!). Now your thoughts have the power to make the personal movie you experience here on earth into a comedy, drama, horror film, suspense thriller, romance, or satire. In any given moment our thoughts are dictating the type of film we're creating for our own viewing. Now here's the kicker. The motion picture of your life was made manifest by the director of divine creation in perfect form before you got here. Your motion picture is spectacular beyond anything you or I could ever dream up. Your role as director is not to complete, improve upon, or even make manifest anything really. The reality of your dazzling movie is already headlining at the cineplex of the universe. It's friggin' sensational! Your playing director here on earth is for your own learning, involvement in the process, and for your entertainment value. Your success and contribution to the universe was already made manifest before you even arrived here. If we however, we want to enjoy the process of directing our movie, and co-creating something we're delighted to see each day while we're here, it would benefit our experience if we generate high frequency thoughts. Abraham Hicks, author of *The Law of Attraction*, writes, "You do not have to work at your higher vibration. Higher vibration, purer vibration, is natural to you. But you do have to let go of the thought that is holding you down."

Living a fearless life is absolutely possible. In fact, we've been sent an open invitation. I know this to be relevant in both of our lives now. For me to write this book and for you to invest in reading it and working to absolve fear and optimize love in your life. We both recognize this on a deep level to be the true.

A fundamental elevation in belief systems and change in our attitudinal response to life is a paramount. Dr. David Hawkins, author of *Power Versus Force*, writes, "It is said in Alcoholics Anonymous that there is no recovery until the subject experiences an essential change in his personality. This is the basic change first manifest by AA founder Bill W.—A profound transformation in a total belief system with a sudden leap of consciousness. Such a major metamorphosis in attitude was first formally studied by American psychiatrist Harry Tiebout who discovered, while treating a hopeless alcoholic woman named Mary. She was the first woman in AA. She underwent a sudden change of personality to a degree unaccountable through any known therapeutic method. Dr. Tiebout documented that she was transformed from an angry, self-pitying, intolerant, and egocentric posture to a kind and gentle one. She became forgiving and loving. Her example is important because it so clearly demonstrates this key element in recovering from any progressive or hopeless disease. (The disease of fears.) Dr. Tiebout wrote the first of a series of papers on this observation under the title, *The Power of Surrender*. Once again, the validity of surrendering, trusting the flow of life, and the intelligence of the larger design is reflected in schools of study throughout philosophy, spirituality, science, and medicine alike. The key element here is that we surrender control and raise the quality of our thoughts so we can align with the highest quality of life; the life that was intended for us before we were even born. Nothing in the universe can keep us from experiencing a kind, gentle, forgiving, and loving life except perhaps, our own self-limiting thoughts. Our capacity to surrender is interwoven with our capacity to trust. When we lay our heads down to go to sleep each night, we trust that the sun will come up the next morning. Sure, some days it is not as bright. Some days the light is covered by clouds or fog. Sometimes the light is blocked by trees grown so tall it is hard to see beyond them. But, rest assured dear friend, the sun will keep its promise. It will rise.

Practice:

I find that to stay in the realm of high frequency thoughts it is compulsory that we give ourselves permission to be of the belief system that the universe is indeed conspiring with us to support our highest good. Which is to say basically, the proverbial, "If it's meant to be, it will be." Everything that's happening is happening for a reason. If we're seeing something as chaotic or out of alignment with our highest good, it's because we're not seeing it clearly.

Power Versus Force reads, "Nonlinear dynamics has verified that there really is no chaos in the universe; the appearance of disorder is merely a function of the limits of perception." And if we trust this to be true, then we can surrender. We can soften our grip, micromanagement, and inordinate attachment to our thoughts. Our thoughts are here to color an already perfect experience. The only thing that can blemish the experience is adhering to the thought forms that do not support the enjoyment of the experience. I find that when I become disgruntled or even swept into emotional turmoil by an experience, with the passage of time, I come to learn that it was that exact experience that I fought so hard against that brought me to more elevated place. Imposing fear-based control mechanisms, which are low frequency thoughts, onto a situation is basically like injecting a virus into a perfectly healthy organism; when indeed we could just play in the space that is indeed the perfectly healthy organism, which is our life. Assuming rigidity in our thoughts when confronted with a scene in our life we want to control is like assuming an entire book based on one punctuation point. From our current vantage point, we can not know the whole story. We have to trust it's working in our favor. Alan Watts teaches us, "The meaning of life is just to be alive. It is so plain, and so obvious, and so simple. And yet, everyone rushes around in a great panic, as if it were necessary to achieve something beyond themselves." Watts goes on to say, "The art of living...is neither careless drifting on one hand, nor clinging to the past on the other. It consists of being sensitive to each moment, in regarding it utterly new and unique, in having the mind open and wholly receptive." So, here's the practice. Breathe. Breathing helps us soften, relax, and connect to the present moment, which is by the way perfect. And in every moment that we're established with our breath, we're present. The present is always perfect. The breath helps us understand that in any given moment, we're in the perfect place (even if it doesn't logically seem that way at the time). Our breath is our vehicle in which we can travel in peaceful awareness. It is a device that helps us surrender. And if this is new for you, and it seems far fetched, it will at least feel like a chill pill. By taking the "chill pill" of breath work, time will reveal that indeed; this too was meant to be.

How to breathe: Just sit up tall. Straight spine. Shoulders relaxed. Chin level with the earth. First just notice that you're breathing. This is intrinsically calming in of itself. Now, see if you can breathe in and out through the nose.

WE CAN SOFTEN OUR GRIP, MICROMANAGEMENT, AND INORDINATE ATTACHMENT TO OUR THOUGHTS. OUR THOUGHTS ARE HERE TO COLOR AN ALREADY PERFECT EXPERIENCE.

Notice the rhythm and pace of your natural breath. Is it fast or slow? Stable or erratic? Make no judgement either way. Just observe. (The breath is a printout of the mind. Ideally, one day we would like to establish a slow stable breath. This would be an illustration of a stable and calm mind.) For now, inhale for the count of four, 4-3-2-1. Pause. Hold the breath for four counts. 4-3-2-1. Exhale for four counts. 4-3-2-1. Repeat. Inhale 4-3-2-1. Hold the breath. 4-3-2-1. Slow exhale, 4-3-2-1. If you can, breathe in and out only through the nose. This will help calm your nervous system and invoke ease in the mind-body. If you're congested, you can breath through the mouth. No problem. Follow this breath awareness exercise for two to five minutes. (The yogis call it Pranayama; or breath, or energy control. You see, by managing the breath you manage the mind. i.e. You direct the director.) You can do this practice every morning upon rising and again right before bed. It's also safe and effective to practice intermittently throughout the day. Just breathe, just breathe.

CHAPTER EIGHT

The Voices in Our Heads

Story:

AN OLD CHEROKEE chief teaching his grandson about life... "A fight is going on inside me," he said to the boy, "It is a terrible fight and it is between two wolves. One is evil. He is anger, envy, sorrow, regret, greed, arrogance, self-pity, guilt, resentment, inferiority, lies, false pride, superiority, self-doubt, and ego. The other is good. He is joy, peace, love, hope, serenity, humility, kindness, benevolence, empathy, generosity, truth, compassion, and faith. The same fight is going on inside you and every person too." The grandson asked his grandfather, "Which wolf will win?" The chief replied, "The one you feed."

Sitting cross-legged on the carpet of my childhood bedroom floor with vigor and vengeance, I scribbled, "You're ugly. You're fat." onto the pages of an otherwise blank spiral notebook. I was 15. I was writing hate notes to myself. This is when I first became notably aware of the voice in my head. We all have this voice. It's our self-talk, our internal narrative. Deep in the trenches of anorexia, I hated myself and had become a manic generator of vicious thoughts that satiated the bad wolf within. I am not hung up on my story of anorexia. Fear manifest and rears its ugly head in innumerable ways; that just happened to be mine. Anorexia was my teacher. It was loud and relentless. I'm sure the lessons were presented more gently in the years proceeding that disorder, but clearly I wasn't willing to acknowledge the teacher or engage in the assignment until it demanded my absolute attention. The lesson for me was to acknowledge the voice of fear that dwelled within me. I had to recognize its capacity to contaminate my state, inflate my sense of self, and completely separate me from my own Self. I had to learn how to regain my connection to God and the power that lies therein. Perversely negative self-talk sounds like a voice of self-hate; which I appreciate sounds dramatic, but it applies. The terms self-abuse or self-harm could be used as well. Either way, the voice, at least for me, has always been prevalent. Sometimes its damaging cadence takes on a more discrete tone. For example, I'd forget something and think, *You're such a ditz.* I'd send an email before I spell checked it and berate my intelligence. I'd sit by my phone and wait for a text that never came and assume the radio silence was just an accurate confirmation, *It's true, I'm not worthy.* There never seemed to be a shortage of reasons to scrutinize my own existence, and this damn voice insisted on putting any and every tiny imperfection under a microscope and blaring it through an intercom in my mind. We're all telling ourselves stories all day long. We find and create scenarios to reiterate such tales. A voice or collage of voices in our minds animate our personal monologues through language. Through our thoughts we communicate with ourselves. And the scary, yet exciting thing is... we're listening! We start to believe the voice even if it is nonsensical and cruel. The voice of self-hate is the voice of fear, not love. The voice of self-hate is self centric and terrified. It is an ego-driven voice that won't stop until we are completely separated from God. *A Course in Miracle* states, "God calls you and you do not hear, for you are preoccupied with your own voice." The Course goes on to say, "The voice of spirit is as loud as your willingness to listen." Our unique self-talk shapes our perspective and choices. This self-talk is the most colorful paint brush then can possibly dance across the canvas of our lives. So given all its power, it's striking to realize how little thought we've given it. When caught in a fear-based loop, it's nearly as though the tone was set, and we just function on autopilot while the voice plays in rounds without us even questioning it. We have the power to adjust the whole story. We get to choose the voice that we want to dominate our lives. We get to decide what language will shape our world.

Truth:

Here's the first thing I came to understand: The voice of self-hate is consistently inaccurate.

That evil-intentioned voice such as the one that thundered through my 15-year-old mind while I scribbled in my notebook had horrible manners. It was insanely rude and was absolutely false. Any voice that does not sound loving is not real and can not be trusted. It is our job to recognize and silence the bad wolf for what it is—a scavenger that feeds on vulnerability and places where love is not.

ANY VOICE THAT DOES NOT SOUND LOVING IS NOT REAL AND CAN NOT BE TRUSTED.

No one, not even ourselves through our own thoughts, can offend us without our own consent. By allowing this voice to live in our minds, we are giving it power. The voice of self-hate deserves zero authority, but if we believe it, it has power over our lives. Have you ever noticed how we can receive numerous compliments and one insult; but it's the insult that haunts us? Why? Because we believe it. Words cannot effect us if we do not believe them.

Our first mission is to stop believing the bad wolf. We can silence it by taking away it's platform and overriding any opportunity it may have to speak by replacing those thoughts with the opposite thoughts. Thoughts that are based on scarcity can be placed with thoughts of abundance. Thoughts that are based on fear are instantly drowned out by thoughts that are based on love. The voice of self-hate is an illusion. The voice of love is absolute. Patanjali, the father of yoga, writes in the Yoga Sutras, an ancient text on yoga philosophy, "Vitarka-Badhane-Prati-Paksa-Bhavanam," or "When disturbed by disturbing thoughts, stop and think the opposite." As a young girl, I had to become aware of this destructive voice and it's motivation to feed the bad wolf to sustain itself. I had to understand where this voice came from and why my mind had become a dwelling place for such cruelty. Fear had to get loud enough for me to listen. And so I did. What I came to realize is that the only reason fear abided within me with such magnitude is because I didn't have enough self-love. Self-love makes the mind inhabitable to fear. Fear is an opportunist. Where love is absent, fear thrives. Deep beneath the surface of an otherwise good enough life, a severe lack of self-love had been coursing through my veins and actively hijacking my life. It started in my teen years and haunted me into adulthood. I had to put a stop to this needless harm. Deficiencies in self-love are not always ostensible. Symptoms of inadequate self-love often reside within the most private chambers of one's life. That's part of the problem. If someone has a visible wound, people around them offer bandages and aid. If someone is physically hurt, we take precautions not to cause further discomfort. But self-hate is invisible. The person who can offer the greatest relief is both the inflictor and the inflicted. If you saw me walking down the street, I'd probably look a lot like you. Confident enough, happy enough, smart enough... nothing lacking or out of place. But just like you, I have an internal monologue that, left to its own devices, can be malevolent when it's in a mood. This internal monologue plays out as the proverbial good wolf, who sees the world from a vantage point of love in battle with the bad wolf, who sees the world through a lens of fear. In order to overcome the source of pain, we have to acknowledge it and look it square in the eye. *A Course in Miracles* teaches us that a miracle is a shift in perception from fear to love. I wish I would have known how to shift my perspective from fear to love when I was 15 years old, but had I not suffered then, I wouldn't be here now. So, while I'm grateful for that lesson, I wish to impart it onto anyone who may be assaulting the Self. *A Course in Miracles* says, "When you want only love you will see nothing else." It is our job to keep our minds fixated on love. See love, speak love, hear love, be love—desire only love; know that you are love. It is through self-love that we successfully starve the bad wolf.

SELF-LOVE MAKES THE MIND INHABITABLE TO FEAR. FEAR IS AN OPPORTUNIST; AND WHERE LOVE IS ABSENT, FEAR THRIVES.

Practice:

Mindfulness exists when we encapsulate our thoughts, experiences, and actions with awareness.

Awareness is the bedrock of mindfulness and the catalyst for all healing. Mindlessness makes us easy targets for fear. Complacent and extraneous mental chatter is easily snatched up by the fangs of fear. We don't want to give the bad wolf the bait. Mindfulness can fill voids where love is absent and evict self-hate before it has a chance to move in. Mindfulness entails that we are conscious of our thoughts, and use discernment in which thoughts persists and which thoughts pass by without taking effect. Being mindful does not mean that we become compulsive about managing and manufacturing the "right" thoughts. We have nearly 60,000 thoughts a day. It would be intractable to expect all of these thoughts to be positive and universally helpful. Our internal narrative will always be varied and nuanced. The first step to mindfulness is becoming a witness to our thoughts. We don't have to directly change them right away. Just by witnessing our thoughts, we'll have a heightened ability to uncover tendencies and patterns that may be blocking the insurmountable love we could be giving ourselves. To help me with this process, I often visualize my thoughts as being on a conveyor belt. As the watcher of my thoughts, I float over the conveyor belt and survey the thoughts as they pass by. When I spot a thought that does not contribute to my wellbeing or the wellbeing of others, I flick it off. The thought just disappears.

AWARENESS IS THE BEDROCK
OF MINDFULNESS, AND THE
CATALYST FOR ALL HEALING.

This visualization started out as an experiment, but has proven helpful in illustrating the impermanence of my thoughts. We get to decide what is worthy of our attention. Fear-based thoughts are distractions, not reality. So, sit or lie down and close your eyes. Make sure your physical body is comfortable. Your spine should be in a straight line. Soften your eyes, cheeks, and jaw. Let yourself rest. There is nothing to do; just notice the thoughts that come to mind. If any disturbing thought arise, acknowledge that thought and dismiss it by shifting your focus to the next thought. If the next thought is also disturbing, replace that thought with an opposite one. For example, if you think, "The tag on my shirt is scratching me. I'm uncomfortable. This is a waste of time." Kindly acknowledge that thread of thoughts and move on. If the subsequent thought is, "No, it's super itchy and I have things to do." Gently replace that thought with, "I am safe and comfortable. I am where I am meant to be." Allow this exercise to be a practice in cultivating awareness, harnessing mindfulness, and learning how to steer the conversations in your mind to becoming harmonious and pleasant.

Dear voice of 'I am not enough',

I have not had enough of you. I welcome you in. I invite you to dwell in the loving nest of my heart. Get cozy. Slip off your defenses. Turn down your criticism. I know you must be exhausted from the long day you've had. I know how draining judgment can be. Let me nourish you. Let me fill you up. Allow me to reinforce your strengths. The content we'll work on, but I applaud your voice, your willingness to speak up, and your dedication to your cause. Yes, dear voice of, 'I am not enough', you've been gravely misguided. You're fighting yourself, you see. I'm here to hug you and hold you; to remind you that you're part of me and I love all of me. Voice of 'I am not enough', I love you, and you are enough. You can rest now, if you please.

CHAPTER NINE

Fear

Story:

I WAS IN Albuquerque, New Mexico taking a summer intensive with my favorite Ayurveda teacher, Dr. Vasant Lad. Classes were in session each day from 10:00 a.m. to 5:00 p.m., which meant I had the mornings and evenings to be outside. The skies in New Mexico are ballooning in volume and height. That atmosphere seems fuller than it does in Florida. While the arid climate is mostly dry and flat, there is a majestic thread of rolling hills and small mountains known as the Elephant Mountain.

It's called this because the silhouette of the rock formations resemble the head of an elephant. Hiking through the trails, surrounded by cactus and various desert foliage and being swallowed by the exaggerated Western skies, brought me tremendous peace. One evening, just a couple hours before sunset, I was strolling along in silence. The sound of my tennis shoes on the gravel was the only sound in my ear shot. On this particular late afternoon I was in complete solitude on the path. I must have walked for over an hour without seeing a single other soul. The path was distinct. Prior hikers had highlighted the walking trail with footprints and flattened weeds. But somehow on this day, I lost my way. It was when I found myself in a shallow sand ditch that the silence was replaced by the vivid sounds of rattling. My heart skipped a beat. I looked directly down. Nothing. As my eyes bolted straight ahead, there she was. A long, thick, and active rattlesnake just three feet away. This is going to sound wild, but years prior while in India a Jyotish reader, or Indian astrologer told me that I would encounter a vicious dog in Indonesia (that never happened by the way), and various wild animals throughout my life. He instructed me that when I do I should mentally place the animal in a pink bubble and chant "Loka Samastah Sukhino Bhavantu." This means may all beings everywhere be joyful and free. Essentially, the pink bubble and chanting technique is a mystical approach aimed at a practical outcome: keep calm and stay in the headspace of love, not fear. That evening in the desert that advice jumped into my heart and I did just that. In my mind, the rattlesnake slithered through a huge pink bubble that I placed around it. I silently chanted, Loka Samastah Sukhino Bhavantu, as I slowly walked backwards and away from the snake. Once at what I presumed to be a safe distance, I turned my back to the snake, hoisted one of my legs onto a ledge, and crawled out of the sand ditch. Phew! But the evening of being tested by fear didn't end there. I continued hiking along as the blue sky shifted into a deep purple with a gorgeous orange ribbon just above the horizon. I felt so peaceful.

Then, I saw a wolf. Yes, a wolf. I was sure of it. He was about three feet in height. He had an athletic frame, gray fur, black ears, and piercing blue eyes. *Fuck!!!* That's what screeched through my head. Internally, I had a brief moment of sheer panic.

The pink bubble of light and the calming chant was cute and all for the rattlesnake. I suppose with the snake I assumed I could run faster or leap higher. I had height and two legs on my side. But with a fucking wolf? Oh my God!!! Then in one breath, something changed. I recalled an episode I watched on NatGeo, *When Animals Attack*. I remembered a few useful tips. 1. Never make eye contact. 2. Keep your ears open. 3. Pretend to be calm. 4. Wolves will go for your ankles for their first point of contact. With these nuggets of insight (backed up by zero experiential evidence by the way), I took a deep breath, looked down at my feet, slowed my pace, and repeated, "I love you life. Thank you for this life. I love you life. Thank you for this life. I love you life. Thank you for this life." Don't get me wrong, one level of my being was still scared shitless, but another level of my being was at peace with whatever was about to happen. What I can imagine to be about a minute later I heard a jingly sound right next to me. I looked to my right and there was a beautiful and friendly husky wearing a dog collar. The collar was the jingling. I was ecstatic. Elated. Every cell in my being was engulfed with peace, joy, and supreme gratitude. The extreme irony here is that up until that moment I was actually a little fearful of dogs (mostly because the Indian astrologer told me I would be attacked by a vicious dog several years prior.) Can you believe it? Either my insane human mind saw a dog and transmuted it into a wolf based on fear-based programming, or perhaps my conviction to stay in a pure and uninterrupted state of love transformed a wolf into a dog. Okay, the latter is probably less likely; but either way that eventful afternoon taught me that we are given unlimited opportunities in life to be scared shitless or engulfed in love. That evening in the New Mexico desert taught me that from my personal experience I did and will always benefit more from operating at a level of love over a level of fear.

Truth:

Fear is love that has been turned upside down. Fear is love that is gravely disoriented. Fear is the opposite of love. Fear communicates only through means of the small (s) self. Fear attaches itself to the small self and manipulates it into thinking it's not enough. Fear causes us to judge, compare, criticize, condemn, build walls, and attack. Like with the wolf in Albuquerque, fear causes us to see things not as they are, but as we fear them to be.

ANYTHING THAT IS NOT LOVE IS A REQUEST FOR LOVE.

Fear works internally so we commit these crimes against ourselves (like my battle with anorexia nervosa), as well as outwardly towards others. Fear projects false perceptions onto ourselves and others in insidious ways (such as making an innocent 15-year-old girl believe she's not worthy of existing the way she was. Fear led me to believe I needed to be different than I was in order to be worthy.) Fear is steadfast in its mission to convince us of lies. Fear is how an inflated ego survives. If we think we're not good enough, we have to either belittle others to appear big or force ourselves into positions of prestige and status—often through disingenuous means. That or we condemn ourselves into corners of unhappiness resolute in a belief that fear is right, "We're just not good enough."

Fears objective is to keep the big (S) Self in the shadows because fear knows it cannot coexist with the magnificence of Self.

Self is love. Fear and love cannot coexist. *A Course in Miracles* teaches us, "Every choice you make is either an expression of love or an expression of fear. There is no other choice." I know that was a lot to take in. And my guess is that you are no stranger to the many faces of fear. Anytime you felt unworthy, less-than, arrogant, better-than, unresponsive to receiving love, overindulging and desperate in giving love, isolated and alone, anxious, depressed, angry, or vengeful—that was fear. It all boils down to this: In any given moment, our immediate and active response to life is coming from one of two places: fear or love. Here's our barometer: love feels peaceful. Fear is saturated in discontent. Consider this: anything that is not love is a request for love. This voice in our heads that sound like fear is starving for love. It's a terrified voice. This is the voice of self-hate. Fear itself is scared, that's why it's such a bully. It knows that without its manipulating tricks it would be annihilated by love. Love is so much stronger than fear, but until we figure this out and believe it, it lives within us. We are just a host. Fear is a parasite and while it's present, it hides behind various masquerades to keep itself safe. Envy, insecurity, greed, comparison, criticism, and judgment are all costumes of fear.

Society and consumerism as a whole reinforce reasons to perpetuate the costumes of fear because its profitable. Media teaches us to feel incomplete and inadequate because self-hate is outrageously lucrative. Anti-aging and weight loss are multibillion dollar industries. I won't hop on a soap box here, but propaganda that commemorate prejudice towards ourselves and others are building blocks for capital. It is our moral obligation and prerogative to recognize lies and make choices with our wallets and minds that advocate truth. We are good enough. We don't need to literally buy into fear. I'm pretty sure the economy will be just fine, even when you and I decide we don't need cosmetic surgery or expensive cars to prove our worth. We are worthy as we are. With that being said, if we choose to partake in cosmetic surgery, luxury items, or whatever it may be that's absolutely valid. It should just be a choice that comes from conscious thought and confident desire, not a choice made for us through poisonous fumes of societal fear. So as it seems, choosing love over fear is a choice. It would appear the first step in making the choice that brings us peace (love), over discontent (fear) would be in recognizing the symptoms of fear (essentially anything that doesn't feel harmonious), and then taking the necessary actions to align ourselves with love. The necessary action might be as simple as a shift of thought, a change in environment, having an intentional conversation, or maybe even distancing ourselves from the person or thing that is triggering our fear. Distancing ourselves from the person or thing that is triggering our fear does not mean that we label the source as toxic and righteously proclaim are elevated status as being "above" toxicity. Doing so would be counterintuitive.

Proclaiming we're better than someone or something is a coercive tactic of fear itself. Remember, no one can make us feel anything without our consent. We are autonomous creatures. The fear is our own if we choose to allow it to exist within us. We cannot blame anyone else for our fear. Wayne Dyer tells a story that illustrates this well. To paraphrase, 'You can squeeze an orange by hand. You can use an electric juicer. You can even poke a straw through it and suck the juice out. It's not how the orange is manipulated that determines what's inside. No outside influence can create the contents inside the orange. What comes out is what's inside. In the case of an orange, it's orange juice. The same is true for you and I. We can be poked, prodded, hugged, squeezed real tight, or triggered. But in any case, what comes out is what was inside.'

We are responsible for our contents. When we feel symptoms of fear, we are responsible for how we respond. If it is a person that is triggering our fear, we can distance ourselves without feeling superior. This distance is an act of self-love, not superiority. If it is something, such as magazines with an array of beauty advertisements, or the news with an extreme amount of violence that is triggering our fear, we can choose to close the magazine or turn the TV off. Again, not with an attitude of righteousness, but rather the recognition that it is not right for us.

These are examples of ways to turn towards love rather than fear.

BUT SOMETIMES THE WISEST INVESTMENT WE CAN MAKE IS TO LOVE THOSE WHO ARE DIFFICULT TO LOVE. BECAUSE BY GIVING THEM SOMETHING THEY ARE LACKING, IT AWAKENS WITHIN THEM THE CAPACITY TO PERPETUATE WHEN THEY'VE JUST BEEN AFFORDED.

I experienced a personal caveat here, as I write this chapter. I'm currently in Cuba. I came here with the intention of sourcing inspiration from this colorful culture in efforts to funnel that inspiration into my writing. Cuba and the people here are both colossally bright and kind. I love it here very much. What happened was not indicative of Cuba. This could have happened anywhere in the world. This morning I was walking around and a beggar asked me for money. Typically, when traveling I intentionally invest in the country through my tourism dollars and sometimes choose a reputable organization to make a donation. I rarely give money to beggars on the street for a host of reasons. So as this man approached me, I politely gave him a soft smile and said "no, por favor." He asked again. Again, I gave him the same response. The third time he walked up to me, touched my arm with his right hand and put his begging hand palm up less than an inch from my chest. I yelled, "NO!" Where did my love go? I was consumed by fear. You see, safety seems to be a prerequisite for displaying love outwardly to others. Abraham Maslow's hierarchy of needs begins with safety and basic survival needs. According to the hierarchy of needs, without secured safety, we can not transcend towards self-awareness. The Chakra system of Ancient India mimics this model. The first chakra, or reservoir of energy governs safety and security. If this reservoir of energy is not stabilized, the proceeding energy spheres will not be in balance. What was revealed to me in this setting was that love is not absent in the moment of physical threat, it is just turned inward. In this case, physically distancing myself from the trigger of fear was a mandatory act of my own self-love. I was not unloving towards the man; in that I did not inflict harm upon him or wish him unwell. I just needed to secure my own basic needs in order to absolve any fears surrounding my physical safety. We have to feel physically safe to feel emotionally safe.

This morning reminded me that it is easy to speak about love and behave lovingly when afforded the luxury of a safe and loving ecosystem. But when physical threat and imminent danger are very real elements in an environment, the call to love is layered with complexities. This is where I ask questions that I myself do not have distinctly accurate answers to, for my perspective can be based only on my own social conditioning, cultural landscape, and personal experiences. At best, I can expand my vantage point to imagine what it must be like for people living lives that are indeed a stark contrast to my own. In cases of domestic violence, most developed countries have support networks and agencies in place to help. Without hesitation—reach out immediately. Seeking help is a courageous act of self-love. As for those who face fear manifested through war, and political upheaval, for them I have empathy and love. But no concrete solutions. I can offer this, Jim Carey, who I see as a philosopher on top of being an extraordinary actor, said this in his commencement speech given to the graduating class of 2012 at Maharishi University, "Energy is the most valuable currency." I'd agree, and add that 'Love is the most valuable energy.' As love is the most valuable universal currency, it is worthwhile to invest in love regularly. Think of distributing love as distributing wealth. We each have a love bank account, so to speak. It's logical to want to apply the same principle to love as we do to money. We want to see a return on our investment. It's tempting to love only those who are easy to love and who love us back. But sometimes the wisest investment we can make is to love those who are difficult to love. By giving them something they are lacking, it awakens within them the capacity to perpetuate what they've just been afforded. Withholding love first and foremost to our own-selves and then to others does not inflate it's value. We don't gain strength by denying or hoarding love. Withholding love depreciates the value of our own energy and the overall value of energy on the planet because love has value based on a belief system. Contributing to our love accounts reinforces our collective trust in the system. Giving love to others provides them with gains. Giving love to people especially who are difficult to love is furthermore a grand investment because it affords them the ability to see value in something they themselves have grown skeptical to trust. The old adage, "Hurt people, hurt people." is often used by psychologist and is popular for a reason. It makes sense. People who are hard to love are typically this way because they are hurting. They are often hurting because they do not feel loved. In the absence of love, they have lost trust in it's value. They've stopped investing. By giving them love, you remind them that they still have an open account and available worth. Sharing love is like trading in the stock market. The more people who are involved, the stronger the system.

Let's use money as a tangible example. The anthropological book, *Sapiens* informs us that the sum total of money in the world is about 60 trillion dollars, yet the sum total of money in bank notes and coins is about 6 trillion dollars. More than 90 percent of money that appears in accounts exists only in computers. That means on a daily basis, billions of people all over the world are exchanging goods and services, not for tangible currency, but rather for a shared belief that the value exists. Anthropologist and historian Yuval Noah Harari of *Sapiens* wrote, "Money is the most universal and most efficient system of mutual trust ever devised." When people place their trust in something, such as money, (or LOVE) they structure their life to operate around it. Imagine a world that operates around a trust in love.

THE QUESTION ITSELF CREATES SPACE BETWEEN THE THOUGHT, FEAR, AND REALITY. THE QUESTION 'DO I KNOW THIS TO BE TRUE?' GIVES US PERMISSION TO OFFER OURSELVES GRACE.

Practice:

For most of us, the majority of our fears are in our heads. And as we have determined, our heads are not the most accurate breeding grounds for reality.

This method is designed to give space between the thought and the response, and in that space we can examine if the fear based thought can even hold water. To practice this method, we pose a question, "Do I know this to be true?"

Going back to my 15-year-old self who thought, *I'm fat! I'm ugly!* Had I known then what I know now, I could have posed the question, "Do I know this to be true?" There is no way on God's green earth the answer could have been yes. *I'm fat and I'm ugly* were nothing more than temporal thoughts, drowning in fear, erroneously pronouncing psychobabble in a desperate attempt to stay afloat. There is zero truth behind the thoughts that haunt us. As a little girl, I likely attacked myself because fear attacked me. The question in itself creates space between the thought, fear, and reality. The question, "Do I know this to be true?" gives us permission to offer ourselves grace. Any thought that feels like an assault on ourselves or another is a thought that needs grace. So next time you catch yourself caught up in a story line that breeds envy, insecurity, greed, comparison, criticism, or judgment ask yourself, "Do I know this to be true?" Next time you mistake the proverbial dog for the proverbial wild animal, ask yourself, "Do I know this to be true?" Fear loves us to see what doesn't exist because if we're scared, we're distracted. When we're distracted we're in the ego's world. When we're in love, we're present. When we're present, we're in the world of Soul.

CHAPTER TEN

Weapons of Fear: Comparison & Judgement

Story:

REMEMBER HOW I said part of unleashing the shackles of fear would feel uncomfortable and we'd be tempted to sweep the ugliness under the rug or skim past it? For me, this is that moment. Thinking, talking, and certainly writing about comparison and judgment spark within me a heavy feeling of supreme tribulation. Probably because I am so keenly aware of the frequency in which I've tortured myself by enabling these two faculties of fear to wrap their tentacles around my mind and actions in such a way that all my insecurities were squeezed to the surface. I've realized over the years that comparison is a preeminent cause of suffering and that judging someone says little to nothing about the subject being judged and reveals a lot about me. Comparison and judgment once occupied common place in my life. With experience and wisdom, they are faculties of my past, but even to sit and write about these themes did reawaken the memory of the pain they have caused me. I don't need to tell you how easy it is to partake in this self-sabotage game. It is the job of Self to rise above it. Comparison is a normal function of the brain. It's human nature to categorize things. This brain function protected the human species; these plants are bitter, don't eat them. They're poisonous. These plants by contrast are sweet. Eat them. They're nutritive. This sort of sorting is healthy. But when we start to categorize elements, mainly people into categories of good and bad, right and wrong, better than and worse than, we have lost the heart of why we're here. We're here to learn to love. It is not our job, and actually does a disservice to our job, to spend time and energy establishing hierarchies based on comparison and judgement. It's too easy to compare and judge. The temptations to do so are far reaching. However, the result of such thinking is pernicious and moves us away from love rather than towards it.

WHEN WE START TO CATEGORIZE ELEMENTS, MAINLY PEOPLE INTO CATEGORIES OF GOOD AND BAD, RIGHT AND WRONG, BETTER THAN AND WORSE THAN, HOWEVER, WE HAVE LOST THE HEART OF WHY WE'RE HERE.

I know for me, anytime I catch myself comparing and judging it is because I am in my ego-thinking mind. An atmosphere of fatigue and restlessness create cracks in the foundation of Self. The ego is an opportunist, behaving like a vulture pining for our weak spots. It searches for the spaces where we have momentarily forgotten the Self. The ego can all too swiftly sweep in and alter our mindset.

For example, and this really happened. I was coming off a long day. I felt disconnected from my Self because I didn't make time to eat wholesome food, which made me feel tired and heavy. I didn't receive as much gratitude from clients as I'm accustomed to. The yoga pants I grabbed were too tight, and I was carrying guilt from pulling out in front of someone in traffic. These little things compounded into a bigger issue. I felt frazzled and insecure. The Self is a place of composure and confidence. Frazzled and insecure are residents of the ego. On a day like this, my mind may meander throughout my yoga practice. I might look around the room and compare myself to others in the class. I might wobble in a pose and criticize myself for not being as "good" as I know I could be. This kind of mental activity is unnecessary and exhausting. Frankly, it's B.S.! Comparison and judgement are faculties of fear and as we know, fear is an opportunist. The conditions that move us away from love are the places where we've lapsed in taking care to ground the Self and see ourselves and everyone around us as alleys; perfect individuals who have come together to contribute and share in this human experience.

We want to repeatedly choose thoughts and actions that nourish our energy and capacity to love ourselves and others. Comparison and judgement are the anti-nutrients of thoughts. They are depleting. The practice of shifting away from such draining mental decoys is a true practice; it requires a concerted effort and dedication. I've spent the last decade trying to master this practice. On occasions where I catch myself stepping toward the rabbit hole of negative thoughts, I pause and take a few deep breaths. These breaths escort the small (s) self back into the more capable hands of the big (S) Self.

WHAT WE NEED TO UNDERSTAND IS THAT THERE IS ONLY ONE OF US HERE; WE JUST HAPPEN TO BE IN DIFFERENT BODIES. WE ARE SHARING ONE SOUL; ONE ENERGY SYSTEM; ONE CONSCIOUSNESS.

Taking deep, rich breaths is an instant and effective way to ground and connect to Self. Once I'm able to connect with Self, the ego mind loses its power and I regain mine. Comparison and judgment have little authority over the mind that is securely attached to the Self. Comparison and judgement are self-defeating because no matter how capable we are there will always be someone who is excelling at a faster rate or is just further along than we are. No matter how much money you have, someone else will be richer. No matter how beautiful you are, someone else will be even more stunning. No matter how successful you are, someone else will hold more prestige. You get the idea. And to that, someone else who seems better to you, there's someone else better in their eyes as well. Eyes that look to compare and judge will always find ways to fulfill their desire to compare and judge. If you want to be miserable, there will be people and experiences to satisfy your wanting. So why on earth should we allow our minds to perpetuate a continuum of thought that provides such a disservice?

What we need to understand is that there is only one of us here; we just happen to be in different bodies.

We are all sharing one soul; one energy system; one consciousness. When someone else does well, we do well. When someone else suffers; we suffer. When someone outside ourselves accomplishes their goal or gets a chance to fulfill their dream, we should rejoice. We should rejoice because on a holistic level, we're all connected. There's an enormous energetic web that binds us together. The advancement of one is the advancement of the masses. It's as the truism goes, "We are only as good as the weakest member of the team." It is our function not to compare and judge. We know too well that these thoughts are counterintuitive to our individual happiness and the happiness of the whole.

THE GOAL OF THIS GAME IS TO
LOVE AND SUPPORT EACH OTHER;
TO ADVOCATE FOR ONE ANOTHER'S
HAPPINESS AND WELLBEING.

To heal our tendencies to compare and judge we must understand and believe in the idea of oneness. Two or more people who are competing and judging each other amplify towards war. Two or more people who are loving one another, on the other hand, amplify towards global peace. See, all of these concepts start on an individual and interpersonal level, meanwhile creating a ripple effect that translates in effect to the entire world. Oneness denotes that all the Selves are actually one Self. The only way to experientially embrace this concept is by abandoning the little (s) self that uses comparison and judgement as its attitudinal reflex, and align rather with the big (S) self that seeks to love and be loved in return. John Lennon illustrates this philosophy beautifully in the song, *Imagine*. "Imagine there's no heaven. It's easy if you try. No hell below us. Above only sky. Imagine all the people. Living for today. Imagine there's no countries. It isn't hard to do. Nothing to kill or die for. And no religion too. Imagine all the people, living life in peace. You may say that I'm a dreamer, but I'm not the only one. I hope someday you'll join us, and the world will be as one."

I not only practice yoga, but I teach classes all over the world. On the rare occasion that I catch myself comparing and judging in my personal practice, while taking a class, or while teaching, I breathe and send myself and each person in the room love. As I do this, the negative thoughts vanish. When I see students looking around the room, I often suggest to them that if their eyes wander off their mat and away from their practice to silently send love to the person their eyes wander towards. This is my way of encouraging connectedness. When we connect, we love. When we love, there is no fear. When there's no fear, comparison and judgement are deprived of motive and strength. If you catch yourself feeling tempted to compare or judge, take a deep breath mentally. Say to yourself, I love you. Reinforcing the love within us heightens our capacity to see love and reasons to love in others. Now, see the person nearest to you, in person or in your mind and say to them, "I love you." When we raise our vibration to the height of love, the lower vibrations fall dormant. Comparing in a relationship is a losing paradigm because its sets a stage for expectations. We evaluate our partner against the last partner and expect them to do what the last partner did "correctly," meeting our needs based on XY and Z, but because now we're dealing with a new person, they should be comparably different and even better than the last. They should improve upon the behaviors the previous person conducted that did not meet our standards based on our own erroneous judgments. For example, my first boyfriend Trevor was adoring, but alarmingly irresponsible. I expected my next boyfriend Gram to retain the quality I liked—adorable, but repair the quality that was fractured, responsibility. I learned Gram to be predictable, so then I expected the next person, Bobby to be adoring, responsible, and unpredictable. You guessed it, I learned something about Bobby that I judged to be unfavorable. He wasn't ambitious. So now, the next guy, Mett, needed to be, in my eyes, a composition of all the things I liked and all the things I didn't. I expected Met to be adoring, responsible, unpredictable, and ambitious. You see where this is going. No one wins a game like this. These people did not enter my life to prove to me based on my own tendencies to compare and judge the type of men they were or could become. They were there to be themselves, grow along side me, and teach me about the kind of woman I was and who I could become. What I learned over the decades was that I was the type of person who felt the need to judge people. Largely because I judged myself. What I learned was that I could and have become a woman who does not need to judge. I chose to become a person who does not practice comparison and judgment because frankly, being the type of person who chooses not to engage in such habits makes me happier. Everyone enters our lives at the exact right time to teach as the exact right lesson. They enter in the exact right form. The characteristic of our teachers exist to help us learn to love. The qualities of our teachers are not for our scrutiny, but our growth. Philosopher Alan Watts portrays this eloquently, "We never know how circumstances are going to change and how our need for different kinds of people changes. At one time we may need very individualistic and aggressive people. At another time we may need very cooperative, team working people. And at another time we may need people who are full of interest in dexterous manipulation of the external world. At another time we may need people who explore into their own psychology and are introspective. There is no knowing, but the more variety and the more skills we have, obviously, the better."

The goal of relationships is to love and support each other and advocate for one another's happiness and wellbeing.

THE GOAL OF RELATIONSHIPS IS TO
LOVE AND SUPPORT EACH OTHER;
TO ADVOCATE FOR ONE ANOTHER'S
HAPPINESS AND WELLBEING

The way to excel at being happy in a relationship is to accept and support each other. There is no need to compare yourself to your partner's ex or to other people. No one is as good at being you as you. So be you. Be you fully and wholeheartedly. And allow your partner to be themselves, as they are in the moment. Each moment we are gifted with each other is a gift and deserves to be authentic, free from the blemishes of contrast and criticism. While everyone is worthy of love, it's obviously ridiculous to assume we should love everyone in the same way. This is where discernment comes into play. For example, if you meet someone and realize you have very little interests in common and they seem unenthused in sharing their ideas or seem receptive to yours; then this relationship is starting at a standstill. This type of resistance is indicative of a misalignment. This person is every bit as worthy of love as everyone else, but they might not be attuned to be your friend or partner. To realize this is not comparison or judgment; it is discernment. Send them love and move on. The love you send them is called agape. Agape is defined by the Greeks as a love for the sake of goodness and harmony of humanity.

Not all love has to be personal. When I ended my relationships with Trevor, Gram, Bobby, and Mett I was not wrong in ending the relationships. We were each other's teacher for the exact right moments in our lives and when the lessons were learned, we moved on. Echoes of our relationships stay with us in the form of wisdom. Relationships are a sacred exchange in energy and as Einstein proved, "Energy can neither be created, not destroyed, rather, it can only be transformed." If we're treating people and relationships with the respect they deserve, we see that our teachers accomplish their task to reveal to us enlightened aspects of our selves most effectively by us not comparing and judging them, but by us allowing them to show us what needs to be seen. My error was not in ending my early relationships, but in playing energetic alchemist, blending judgement and comparison to create abstract expectations. Allowing and non-judgement bring us love. *A Course in Miracles* says, "Your task is not to seek love, but merely to seek and find all the barriers within yourself that you have built against it." I know for me, comparison and judgment were my barriers.

ECHOES OF OUR RELATIONSHIPS STAY WITH US IN THE FORM OF WISDOM. RELATIONSHIPS ARE A SACRED EXCHANGE IN ENERGY

Truth:

Spiritual teacher Osho teaches us that, "Comparison is a disease, one of the greatest diseases. We are taught from the very beginning to compare. Your mother starts comparing you with other children, 'Look at Johnny, how well he is doing, and you're not doing good at all.' From the very beginning you are being told to compare yourself with others. This is the greatest disease; it is like a cancer that goes on destroying your very soul. Each individual is unique, and comparison is not possible. I am just myself and you are just yourself. There is nobody else in the world to be compared with. Do you compare a marigold with a rose flower? You don't compare. Do you compare a mango with an apple? You don't compare. You know they are different—comparison is not possible. Man is not a species. Each man is unique. There has never been any individual like you before and there will never be again. You are utterly unique. This is your privilege, your prerogative, life's blessing—that it has made you unique." Fear uses comparison as a mechanism to keep us separate from the whole. The truth is, we are all unique. You are special, but so is everyone else. The Self may use comparison as a mechanism for discernment, such as in our primal state when we think, "That plant is bitter. Don't eat that. That plant is sweet. Eat it. It is nutritious." It's that simple. Discernment keeps us safe. Judgement keeps us separate. It is the false separation that makes us feel crappy because it's based on a lie. Anytime we perceive reality based on an illusion it doesn't feel good. There is no such thing as better than or worse than. The moment comparison turns into a game of hierarchy it is not for the health of the whole. Fear-based comparison creates a gaping gap, a wound that bifurcates us from the harmonious collective. When comparison isolates us from the whole, we become disenchanted with loneliness, isolated to an island of fear, and we suffer. This is a trick of fear. We are too smart and savvy to fall for such cheap ploys. Author Wayne Dyer teaches us to, "Remind yourself that you can not fail at being yourself." Give yourself permission to broaden the perimeters in which you feel worthy and lovable. It is comparison and judgment that we box ourselves into tight, uncomfortable, and unrealistic spaces in which we deem ourselves unworthy of love. Make the boarder so large that you can know that you are worthy and lovable all the time. Your worth and lovability are not based on conditions. Comparison and judgment are pregnant with conditions. When we stop comparing ourselves to each other and who we were yesterday, fear loses its power and judgmental thoughts towards ourselves and others cease to exist. Judgment comes from the ego mind, and as we know the ego mind can not be trusted. Dr. Dyer reminds us, "The only difference between a flower and a weed is judgement."

YOUR WORTH AND LOVABILITY
ARE NOT BASED ON CONDITIONS.
COMPARISON AND JUDGMENT ARE
PREGNANT WITH CONDITIONS.

And one more thing on this topic: Comparing two positives does not equate to a multiplied positive. For example, say you're on vacation in Cuba and you're loving it. You're enjoying the turquoise water, calypso music, and passionately colorful culture, but then you start thinking about the vacation in Italy you enjoyed years prior. You become nostalgic in your mind over the rolling hills of Tuscany, the warmth of the red wine, and the smooth olive oil on your lips. Now you start to compare the brilliance of Cuba with the brilliance of Italy. This sort of comparison is the clever ploy of the ego. The ego mind will try to create traps that lure us away from the here and now; traps that rob us of the joy inherent in the present. The present moment is a place of joy. Joy is death to the ego, so you can bet your ass it will be a kill-joy whenever possible. Be vigilant. The ego depends on complacency of the Self. But when the Self is watchful, the ego backs down. Stay sharp. Stay present. Stay perfectly aware of the moment. When you're absorbed in the positive and the temptation to compare the positive to another positive comes to the surface; pause, take a deep breath and say, "I am here now." Smile and carry on.

Practice:

This practice has several components: Comparison and judgment create a mentality of scarcity; a sense of lacking. For example, if she has more money than me, I have less. If he has received more praise than me, I receive less. This kind of thinking is not fun. This kind of thinking robs us of joy. The centerpiece of love is joy, and joy is bountiful. With a proclivity to compare and judge comes a tendency to see what's missing versus what's there. If you're comparing two plates of food and one has more than the other, instead of seeing one plate as missing a few extra bites of goodness, why not see both plates as an offering of plentiful yummy nourishment? This shift in thinking generates joy, abundance, and love.

1. Dr. Dyer offers us this tool as a practice in non-judgment: "Make a conscious decision to look for what is right and pleasing in others (and your Self). Create a new habit of complementing those around you. Turn judgements into blessings."

2. Comparison and judgement target spaces in our lives where we're disconnected from the Self. Be vigilant. Observe spaces where comparison and judgment tend to surface. As they surface, notice them and replace them with the affirmation, "I have unconditional permission to experience joy."

3. If the ego mind starts to involve other people in the paradigm of comparing and judging, pause, take a deep breath and say, "I love you," first to yourself. Then say, "I love you," to the other person, or people involved. Watch the shift. You'll feel it at a visceral level. Your shoulders may relax, your jaw may unclench, and your body temperature may even change.

4. If you catch yourself comparing two positive experiences: pause, take a deep breath, and say, "I am present, and in this presence there is only love."

CHAPTER ELEVEN

Perfectionism

Story:

TONY ROBBINS SAYS, "Perfectionism is fear in fancy shoes." Being an overachiever, highly ambitious, and effective person dominates our current cultural landscape. The incessant attitude of More! Better! Faster! Harder! Hustle! is the disease of our culture. The word disease can be broken down into two parts: "dis", disconnect, and "ease", harmony. A disease is a disconnect from harmony. Perfectionism sharply severs our human sense of harmony and integration with nature.

Nature is not a type-A perfectionist because, frankly, she needn't be. Nature knows perfection in the effortless from sunrise to sunset, winter to spring, and summer to autumn. Nature is the embodiment of right rhythm; the perfect balance of effort and ease. Lao Tau teaches us, "Nature does not hurry, yet everything is accomplished." The Vedas teach us, "Do less. Accomplish more." These ancient teachers understood that doing more, or trying to be more, does not always add value. Value is intrinsic in being who we are, where we are; everything that is meant to be done will be done. In relationships, this means showing up as our complete, and authentic selves, "flaws" and all. The truth is our so called flaws are the freckles of perfection that give us dimension and character. Trying to be perfect has a counterintuitive effect. It turns our character inside out, hiding our God-given true colors that were gifted to us so we could walk through this world as multidimensional beings. Perfectionism not only stresses us out, it makes us bland. I grew up in a loving home and by that I mean I always felt loved. But my childhood, like all others, wasn't without its faults. I came from divorced parents. As a seven year old, I watched my mom calculate the monthly budget and quit smoking because she couldn't afford cigarettes. My childhood wasn't a Hallmark movie, but it was good. I lived in a safe neighborhood. I spent most of my free time running around and making up dances with my best friends, Ashley and Katie. My parents set aside money to send me to weekly dance classes.

THE TRUTH IS, ARE SO CALLED FLAWS ARE THE FRECKLES OF PERFECTION THAT GIVE US DIMENSION AND CHARACTER.

My dad worked in marketing at Disney, so I went to theme parks on the weekends. My siblings and I were close and enjoyed playful sibling banter. It was nice. Hard work was always of high esteem in our house; particularly at my mom's house. My mom is an ambitious, type-A woman. She is a broker at a real estate corporation. She came from very modest beginnings. Her parents couldn't afford to send her to university, so completing her degree was something she had to work hard for. She placed that importance on her children. We didn't have to excel with phenomenal grades, but she, like many people viewed traditional education as a gateway towards success. Success can mean any number of things to any number of people. For some, success is becoming valedictorian at Stanford; for others it's traveling the world and seeing all seven continents.

Success in our home seemed through my youthful eyes to be largely dependent on status and beauty. To no fault of her own, my mother has always been a beautiful woman. Somewhere along the line in her personal journey of growth and discovery, she learned that optimizing this beauty provided her with the confidence she needed to make a name for herself in her business and personal universe. As a child, I noticed that my mom watched her weight, carefully applied make-up, dressed impeccably, and kicked ass at work. She seemed to always be winning awards and earning promotions. The stories we create in our minds as children are often skewed by our narrow vantage point and innocent girth of understanding. But I learned by watching that I needed to place value on beauty and status.

Status as a child meant being popular. I had tons of friends; genuine, joyful, and innocent; but I also "worked" on making friends and being known. I joined student council, after school activities, and clubs such as the broadcast journalism news team to gain notoriety. From my myopic view of the world, being popular meant I was successful. I learned how to polish this success by talking about "cool" topics, staying up to speed on gossip, and saying the "right" things to appease my peers. Slowly but surely, covertly, I was learning how to be a perfectionist. The beauty aspect came to a head during the summer between freshman and sophomore year of high school. I was a happy go-lucky 15 year old. I enjoyed sleep overs, playing seven minutes in heaven, and manhunt at high school parties. I danced. I decorated my room in posters of N-Sync and the Backstreet Boys. I prank called my girlfriends. I was so "normal." Then one day, my friend Katie and I decided we should lose weight for the summer. We were cute teenage girls, as all teenage girls are. There was no need for this thought to take form, but diet pills, slim fast, and Victoria Secret bikinis were all the craze. Somehow this agenda settled into our mindset. The diet, so to speak started out as eating less cookies while watching MTV and drinking diet coke instead of regular coke. It was harmless enough. But a few weeks in I decided to take it to a new level. I restricted my food; counting pretzels and grapes into erroneously decided upon rations. I dropped weight. I gained compliments and these compliments boosted my self-esteem and lead me to think that if losing a little weight is good, losing a lot of weight would be better. The ails of perfectionism had taken hold. Over the course of the summer I lost 15 or 20 pounds. The compliments shifted into remarks of worry and even disgust. My friends were concerned, but didn't know how to breach a constructive conversation with me concerning the issue. I became tired and withdrawn. My energy was weak and my animated personality had fallen flat. Perfectionism had poisoned my colorful spirit and turned it into a muted skeleton of who I once was. I felt the ostensible distance between my friends and I grow. In a matter of months I had become isolated, depressed, and clinically very sick. All in the name of perfectionism.

In the middle of my sophomore year of high school I was walking downstairs when I overheard my parents talking. My mom and stepdad were discussing their need to refinance the house to leverage expenses so that I could be sent to inpatient care for my disease (yes, I had embodied an alarming disconnect from harmony). In that moment I realized how much my actions were affecting my family. I seemed to be okay with sabotaging my own life, but I didn't want to ruin my parents lives as well. I decided right then and there to stop what I was doing and start eating. My parents had been taking me to a therapist and nutritionist for months. Starting the next day, I decided to uncross my arms, sit up, open my ears, and be more receptive and compliant in these sessions. I started eating. I gained weight. Physically, I returned to "normal," but mentally and emotionally my demons remained. I knew that. No one else needed to. Not then. Do not worry, my experience with anorexia was part of my divine journey. Had I not undertaken this experience I may have not become so passionate about yoga, Ayurveda: natural medicine, psychology, the power of thought, philosophy, and the healing arts; essentially all of the concepts I write about in this book and others. Our hardships do not weaken us. If we gather the strength and awareness to overcome them, our hardships become the very points in life that strengthen us. I was pricked deeply by the poison of perfectionism so that I could write about it today. They say that if you whistle past a graveyard you won't hear the ghost. That is to say that if you distract yourself, you won't hear your fears. I don't want to whistle past the ghost. I want to silence the ghost. The ghost is the ego. Perfectionism is a distraction. It is yet again, another mask the ego wears to keep us scared and detached from our true Self: our soul. At the level of Self we are beyond perfect.

Truth:

Lao Tzu states, "Perfection is the willingness to be imperfect." Being imperfect entails that we become vulnerable. Hiding behind perfection might be hunkering down in a sterile and pristinely lit room; but it's still hiding. Perfectionism sentences us to busyness that only serves as a distraction, perpetual dissatisfaction, and in many cases isolation—long hours alone at the gym, at the office, or emotionally removed from natural sensitivities of life because we're steadfast in micromanaging the few aspects we can control. Perfectionism is at its core a fear that latches onto control mechanism because it is terrified of life experiences that may expose its vulnerabilities.

PERFECTION IS THE WILLINGNESS TO BE IMPERFECT.

Vulnerability is at the heart of overcoming the disease ridden quest to be perfect. Researcher Brene Brown speaks of vulnerability, "Vulnerability sounds like truth and feels like courage. Truth and courage aren't always comfortable, but they're never weakness." She goes on to say, "Perfectionism is a self destructive and addictive belief system that fuels the primary thought: If I look perfect and do everything perfectly, I can avoid or minimize the painful experience of shame, judgement, and blame." The truth is perfectionism does not protect us from unwanted emotions. It invites them in. In one's dedicated efforts to be perfect, one winds up shaming, judging, and blaming oneself. They may be "protected" from the outside world, but in the confines of perfectionism, they've been trapped in. And not trapped in with the Self, by the way; the Self would not embark upon a path loaded with land mines. Traveling down the path of perfectionism is like taking a journey and using the ego as a compass. Nothing, no where, no one, not even one's own self will ever be good enough through the eyes of perfectionism. It's treacherous. Brown continues to say, "Perfectionism is a 20-ton shield that we lug around thinking it will protect us, when in fact, it's the thing that really preventing us from being seen and taking flight....Vulnerability is the birthplace of innovation, creativity and change." Being vulnerable cures us from perfectionism because by showing up for life, our relationships, and the pursuits armed with authenticity and cloaked in mistakes and comebacks, we see for ourselves that the world consistently holds up a mirror for us—a mirror that reflects back to us our humanity. At the center of being human, inherent worth and intrinsic value thrive. Why? Because we're alive. We needn't do more. And by the way love, doing less isn't going to be easy. As Brene said, "Perfectionism is an addiction and breaking an addiction isn't a walk in the park." E.E. Cummings wrote, "To be nobody but yourself in a world which is doing its best day and night, to make you everybody but yourself means to fight the hardest battle which any human being can fight. And never stop fighting."

Practice:

THE TRUTH IS, PERFECTIONISM DOES NOT PROTECT US FROM UNWANTED EMOTIONS. IT INVITES THEM IN.

Bob Marley said, "Being vulnerable is the only way to allow the heart to feel true pleasure." Point blank, being a perfectionist is being fake. Being vulnerable is being real. If we're posturing ourselves in inauthentic ways we are inhibiting authentic pleasure. Revealing our true Self will mean, yes, that sometimes we'll need to broach the difficult conversations we've been avoiding. Yes, it will mean that sometimes we say no. That we don't force ourselves into pretty little boxes when our Self would be more joyful at the liberation of saying no to things we've been saying yes to simply because we're aiming for prestige, status, and perfection. The true aim remains the same. Love more. Fear less. We recall now Tony Robbins who said, "Perfectionism is fear in fancy shoes." Saying yes to engagements where you must slip of shiny loafers or stilettos when your Self would be more nourished by bare feet in the grass is like eating a candy bar where the main ingredient is fear, but the label says organic. It's a facade. And facades don't hold up. Eventually they crumble. And when the walls of perfectionism come crumbling down we'll be forced to see everything we've been trying to avoid. And that'll hurt. But what will hurt even more is realizing that within the remains of everything we're scared to look at dwelled the most glorious elements of life that we've been missing out on. That will hurt more. Tony Robbins says, "Stop being afraid of what could go wrong, and start being excited about what could go right." Let your walls crumble down. Our most pleasurable and sacred life is waiting. Let's not delay a moment longer.

Here's the practice: Seeing as vulnerability is the antidote to perfectionism, we'll work on becoming more vulnerable. It starts first with that unsaid conversation that we've been hauling around. We all have one. So often conversations that could have been painless if expressed in the moment become monstrous when held captive in the mind. We ruminate. We make assumptions. We over analyze. Speak. What we'll find most of the time is that once we sincerely express what's been weighing us down, we feel lighter. The monsters come out from under the bed because they were never there. Remember, we all want the same thing. To love and be loved in return. Fear is not innovative. Perfectionism uses the same mechanisms to enhance the ego and weaken the Self as comparison and judgment. They're just turned inward. You'll recall the antidote to comparing and judging is in realizing we're all one. To absolve the ails of perfectionism we realize the same truth. We're all connected. When we expose our vulnerabilities we not only give ourselves access to the genuine and sacred beauty within ourselves; we give other people access as well. Ladened in vulnerable connectivity there is growth, creativity, and the limitless potential to be fully human. Perfectly imperfect. Go ahead and initiate the conversation you've been putting off simple because it might not be the perfect time or it might not go perfectly. Share your microscopic truth. Being vulnerable may be clumsy, it may be messy, it may even involve a few tears, but it will reveal if not to the other person, certainly to you, a deeper and more liberated version of the Self.

CHAPTER TWELVE

Self-Love

Story:

CAN I LET you in on a little secret? This book is the investigative and soulful effect of a single, yet impactful "Oh Shit!" moment of do I really not love myself? This question was followed by a period of deep self-inquiry. The answer came up with clarity and honesty. Yes, sadly, I really do not love myself. Sure, I loved myself on the superficial level. I loved myself when I looked the way I desired, earned the accolades I worked hard for, felt financially stable, felt loved by someone I admired, and so on. But if

I stripped away any esteem around my appearance, material possessions and earnings, and reputation, at the core level of loving myself unconditionally for no other reason than simply, yet miraculously existing, I came up short. Why would a woman who dedicated most of her life to understanding spiritual concepts, investing in healing knowledge, and pouring her spirit into helping others not love herself? Great question. In complete exposure, this book was the result of that question. Here's the fundamental truth: If you are alive, it is your birthright to love yourself. The issue is that life, consumerism, media, naive family and societal influences, the ego, and foremost fear in all its many guises try their damnedest to teach us otherwise. The return to loving ourselves does not require that we "do" anything. The doing was done the moment we entered this incarnation. We are intrinsically lovable and deserve to embrace our own self-love. Everything good in this world: altruism, kindness, compassion, forgiveness, creativity, innovation, expansion, and enlightenment are all systemic of self-love. Without self-love these functions rattle and crack to the natural turbulence of life. I must have heard a thousand times over, various iterations of, "You must love yourself before you can love someone else." But the concept didn't register until recently. How it came to be seems silly and small to me now. I was 33 and single. Despite my love of love, fondness of being in a relationship, extensive dating life, and several meaningful romantic partners, I was still single.

I decided to join an online dating app. First off, it's incredibly difficult to communicate any accurate and meaningful portrayal of yourself in five photos and 100 characters or less, but I did my best. Within a couple of months of joining the app, I went on 15 dates with eight different guys. Clearly, I was a woman on a mission. I was lucky to meet several dignified men who had a lot to offer. They just weren't for me. As one would imagine, I became exhausted. At lunch with a girlfriend, a simple statement planted a seed. "Kristen, from what I know about you, your successful at everything you put your heart into. You seem to be investing a lot of energy in dating right now. If it's not working out, maybe something is missing or it's not the right time." As always, my friend was oozing warmth and sincerity. Being around her feels like snuggling with a cozy blanket. Consistent with her nurturing presence, I knew she only intended the best for me.

Lunch wrapped up, we hugged, and carried on with our days; but the seed stayed with me. I spent that afternoon thinking about what she said, *something's missing. The timing isn't right.* The next day I spoke to another friend, the same concept echoed. "Something is missing." It came to me like I was hit by lightning, "Oh shit! Do I not love myself?" I knew instantly the thought of not loving myself was absolutely ludicrous. A person walking through this world without self-love sounded as insane to me as a person walking around without a heartbeat. Isn't self-love what fuels everything good and right in the world? Don't we have to love ourselves before we can truly love another. Eureka!!! That's it! That's what's missing! I don't love myself! And here's the wild part, I acknowledged this with glee. Don't get me wrong, it's tragic that I didn't love myself, but the fact that I had identified the problem meant that I could now move towards the solution.I knew a solution existed because inside every problem a solution patiently waits. I spent the next period of my life determined to establish an unshakable sense of self-love within my being. At the level of soul, I wanted to assure that the love I carried for myself would never be affected by outside influences. I knew right then and there that for as long as the sun would rise each morning, and the flow of the tides stayed in motion, for as long as I exist, I would love myself through and through. And so it began. So began the quest to understand and dismantle all the lies we've been taught to believe. The lies that cover and smother our indwelling right and inheritance to self-love.

I REALIZED BY EXPERIENCE THAT DAY ON THE BEACH THAT TO WALK THROUGH THIS WORLD WITH SELF-LOVE IS LIKE BEING GRANTED V.I.P. ACCESS TO THE PRESENT MOMENT.

The Sunday following this revelation I woke up and rather than looking at my phone to check emails and messages; I instantly turned it off. Not knowing what I would do with my day, I went to the kitchen and poured myself a cup of coffee. Before the coffee could hit the bottom of the mug I thought, *Go walk on the beach*. Be in silence. With a heaviness in my heart due to my crushing realization, but lightness in my mindset, knowing the worst was behind me, I finished my coffee, threw on my suit, and hit the road for the beach. Halfway to the beach, a spiral of thoughts started to whirl through my mind. Nothing groundbreaking was there. They were the same thoughts I habitually allow. My lips are dry. *Where's my phone? Oh yea, it's off. I'm thirsty. I need to pee…* Something in me clicked and I realized I was having these thoughts to distract myself from the present and the one thought I desperately needed to reinforce. I knew I needed to reprogram my mind. I instantly replaced the litany of inconsequential babble with, I love myself. I spent the entire day alone, walking on the beach in silence. I enjoyed the soft sand under my feet. I admired the turquoise water. I reached down and grazed my fingers at the shoreline. I became desensitized to the texture in the grains of sand, seashells, and the tiny bubbles that foamed where the waves met the beach. Second after second, minute after minute, hour followed by hour, that any thought entered my mind, I immediately replaced it with, I love myself. I became acutely present. I noticed then that the reason so many of us avoid the present is that we don't love ourselves. Alan Watts said, "The reason we want to go on is because we live an impoverished present." The present in the absence of self-love is impoverished indeed. If we love ourselves, the present is perfect. We can be absorbed in it. But if we don't love ourselves, the present is "incomplete" and we must dive into our past or lunge forward into our future to find the one "magic bullet" that will fix the present. You see, we escape the present because without self-love, the present feels unsettling and in desperate need of something. Misguided by flawed thoughts, what do we do? We go rummaging around in the past and fast forwarding to the future in hopes to find something that's hidden in plain sight. Self-love. The thing the present needs is the same thing our life needs: our love. I realized by experience that day on the beach that to walk through this world with self-love is like being granted V.I.P. access to the present moment.

My intuition took me a step further. My skin became warm. Kissed by the sweltering heat, I decided to lie down, facedown on my tummy, on a sandbar. My belly was submerged in a shallow pool of water. I must have looked like I was on drugs, because complete free abandonment of what other people might think overcame me. I began to make snow angels in the sand. I felt the moist sand scrape the undersides of my sweeping arms.

I SAW CLEARLY IN THAT MOMENT
THAT I WAS SCARED OF LOSING LOVE.
I WAS SCARED OF BEING IN LOVE.

Up and down, up and down. I was making angel wings. Still the mantra, "I love myself," echoed like a soundtrack in the back of my mind. My conscious thoughts drifted to a friend. He was telling me about a scuba trip where he went 100 feet deep, and how he is planning a surfing trip to surf a wave that is 100 feet high. I loved the contrast of 100 feet above and 100 feet below.

That's when it occurred to me, I've been 100 feet below several times. I've had my heart broken. I've hit rock bottom with a shattered heart a couple of times in my life. So much so, that I actually wasn't scared of heartbreak anymore. Heartbreak wasn't loaded with uncertainty. I knew intimately the anguish of being emotionally 100 feet below. What I didn't know was the sensation of being 100 feet above. The feeling of being unabashedly elated in unconditional love with myself or another. That was uncharted. That would be new. That's when it hit me, *Oh God, that would be scary.* Another Eureka!!! I saw clearly in that moment that I wasn't scared of losing love. I was scared of being in love. I have been neglecting my capacity to embrace self-love as a perverse security mechanism to keep me "safe" from what scared me. The unknown. Loving fully and unconditionally. For choosing to dismiss self-love would keep me in the familiar territory of ephemeral relationships and predictable heartbreak. I made the decision to choose the unknown. I chose instead to move towards what frightened me most, and I knew self-love was the only way to get there.

Truth:

Marianne Williamson teaches us, "Our deepest fear is not that we are inadequate. Our deepest fear is that we are powerful beyond measure. It is our light, not our darkness that frightens us. We ask ourselves, who am I to be brilliant, gorgeous, talented, fabulous? Actually, who are you not to be? You are a child of God. Your playing small does not serve the world. There is nothing enlightened about shrinking so that other people around won't feel insecure around you. We are all meant to be here to shine, as children do. We are born to make manifest the glory of God that is within us. It's not just in some of us. It's in everyone. And as we let our own light shine, we unconsciously give other people permission to do the same. As we are liberated from our own fear, our presence automatically liberates others." Williamson goes on to say, "Love is what we are born with. Fear is what we learned here...We do not heal the past by dwelling there. We heal the past by living in the present." That's it. That's all we need to know. More so, that's all we need to condition ourselves to believe and embody. Wrapping our minds, and to a larger degree, our hearts around the essential truth and light of this world, which is that we are the light of the world is paramount not only to our own happiness and wellbeing, but it is consequential for the happiness and wellbeing of this world. The ego will unleash its army of fear in all their seductive and pervasive forms if we don't stand our ground. The safest, most elevated grounds to build our life upon, are grounds of self-love. So that my friend, is where we will stand. We will sink our feet deep into the foundations of self-love. We will root ourselves in: our right to be here, our right to be light, our right to be brilliant, gorgeous, talented, and fabulous. Not because that's an aspiration; but because that is who we already are. Oh, it sounds so good. It feels so good to write. It feels amazing to read. Now, and what I know to be true based on practice and experience is, it feels even better to live.

Practice:

"I AM" affirmations are one of the most effective ways to reprogram our minds and shape our belief systems. The subconscious mind is powerful and runs a second train of thoughts in the undercurrents of our conscious thoughts. The subconscious mind comprises of 90 to 95 percent of our beliefs and truths. I AM statements pierce through our conscious thoughts and penetrate into the subconscious mind.

THE EGO WILL UNLEASH ITS ARMY OF FEAR IN ALL THEIR SEDUCTIVE AND PERVASIVE FORMS IF WE DON'T STAND OUR GROUND.

We use I AM affirmations to heal the disease (disconnect from ease) cause by currents of fear that the ego has injected into our minds. I AM statements are more than hopes, wishes, or even prayers. I AM statements are declarations of truth. They're not flimsy statements. They're facts. The practice here is to state, "I AM LOVE. I AM LOVE. I AM LOVE," first thing upon rising in the morning, lastly before bed, and at any period during the day when the mind gets caught up in stories of falsehood, inadequacy, negativity, and pain. Allow "I AM LOVE" to become the mantra that reverberates silently in the background of your mind. Watch over time how reasons and temptations to abandon the present vanish. As we foster self-love the present becomes alluring and nearly inconceivably bypassed.

CHAPTER THIRTEEN

Mirror Work

Story:

MY FIRST EXPERIENCE with mirror work took place when I was 22 years old. I was in India doing my first yoga teacher training course. During a free afternoon, a French women named Karin led a lecture on kinesiology and how emotions imbed into our physical bodies through the gateway of the subconscious mind. Basically, the thoughts we habitually think reside in us as energy spheres. Positive thoughts create positive energy. Negative thoughts create negative energy that can lodge into specific organs and areas within the physical body. The negative energy leads to disease, once again, the disconnect from ease. As we learned and experienced with our body scan, we can identify these negative energies as somatic signals. Kinesiology, or reflex testing, is another way to locate energy. Essentially, everything is energy. Positive energy makes us strong and negative energy makes us weak. Kinesiology is a tool through which a practitioner can determine if something such as a material good makes you strong or weak. For example, if you hold an apple your body will test strong, whereas if you hold a cigarette, your body will inform you that the cigarette makes you weak. The same is true with thought. If you think the word love, your body will reflect that and the thought strengthens you. If you think the word fear, your body will inform you that the fearful thought weakens you. Well during this little lecture, Karin invited me to the from of the classroom. She used my arm to conduct kinesiology and she determined that fear was living in my liver. The fear took the form as the emotion, "indignant." I have sense come to understand all of this.

At the time I didn't grasp the idea of kinesiology. I didn't fully comprehend how emotions affect our physical bodies. I didn't really know what the word indignant meant. Nonetheless, Karin told me in order to release this negative energy sphere that had come about as a result of my fear-based thoughts. I needed to go to the bathroom and stare in the mirror. I was instructed to look beyond the shape of my face and color of my skin. She said I must look directly into my own eyes and repeat, "I love you. I love you. I love you." over and over again until I believed it. I was skeptical, but I excused myself from the lecture room and walked downstairs to the restroom. I did as she told. To my surprise and bewilderment tears welled up and streamed down my face. The more I said, "I love you" to myself, the more I cried. I completely lost track of time. I entered a different state; a state I had never experienced. I don't know how long I was in the bathroom or how many hundreds of times I said I love you. But when the tears finally stopped coming, I stopped. I felt strangely exhausted and refreshed at the same time. I released so many trapped emotions that day. For the first time, I literally stared my fearful thoughts square in the face and replaced them with thoughts of love. I have since practiced mirror work many times. Mirror work is indeed a profound practice for replacing defective subconscious beliefs with beneficial thoughts and beliefs. Mirror work is essentially a tool in which we participate in actively rewiring our neurological processes.

Truth:

Author and publish mogul Louise Hay writes, "Mirror work is the most effective method I've found for learning to love yourself and see the world as a safe and loving place. I have been teaching people how to do mirror work for as long as I've been teaching affirmations. And what are affirmations? Put simple, whatever we say or think is an affirmation. All self- talk, the dialogue in your head is a stream of affirmations. These affirmations are messages to your subconscious that establish habitual ways of thinking and behaving. Positive affirmations plant healing thoughts and ideas that support you in developing self-confidence and self esteem, and creating peace of mind and inner joy. The most powerful affirmations are those you say out loud in front of a mirror. Why? Because the mirror reflects back to you the feelings you have about yourself. It makes you immediately aware of where you are resisting and where you are open and flowing. It clearly shows you what thoughts you will need to change if you want to have a joyous and fulfilling life."

Practice:

The practice is simple; but let me be clear, that doesn't mean it will necessarily be easy. I'd encourage you to explore the exercise and embrace what comes up for you. Simply stand or sit comfortably in front of a mirror. Please look past your outwardly appearance and look deeply into your eyes. Take a deep breath in and a deep breath out to first become present. Then while looking into your own eyes say, "I love you. I love you. I love you." Repeat this at least three times to begin. If you wish to go deeper, set a timer for three minutes and repeat the sentiment until the timer dings. Then once again, take a deep breath in and a deep breath out. You can repeat this exercise daily. As Karin said to me in India, "Repeat it until you believe it."…until you feel it.

CHAPTER FOURTEEN

Vedas: The Five Causes of Suffering

SOMETIME AROUND 400 CE, Patanjali, a man who is said to be, 'the father of yoga' compiled a collection of 196 Indian aphorisms, or scriptures of wisdom into one text titled, *The Yoga Sutras*. Within this book of ancient wisdom, the five main causes of human suffering are delineated and explained. The five causes of suffering are called Kleshas. They are all appendages of fear. Swami Satyananda Saraswati says, "Kleshas are a kind of agony that are inside our very being."

In this section I thought it would be interesting to explore the five main causes of suffering. They are ignorance, aversion, attachment, ego, and clinging to life. I will couple each of the causes with a significant relationship in my life. In writing this, I am presented with a challenge because I will most definitely stay devoted to the philosophical and applicational framework that is vital to our learning and integration of these concepts, while also paying an honorable tribute to the men who came into my life as complete expressions of who they were in that specific period. They taught me genuine, granted sometimes painful lessons. It's important to note for my own conscious and understanding that while from my perspective these men exemplified the specific cause of suffering I'm linking them with here; I too played a role in the turbulence of our experience together. It seems only reasonable to me that these men danced with a specific cause of suffering not because, but in relation to my dance with the same cause of suffering as well. When it comes to relationships and lessons learned in my life, there is no villain and there is no victim. I take full ownership for my part in each of these stories. Each cause of suffering is indeed like a dance, the cha-cha, the waltz, the carlton—each style of suffering required different moves, strategies, and tempos. When the dance was learned, the dancer moved on.

(The names of these men have been changed to respect their privacy.)

My High School Boyfriend: Trevor

Story:

I WAS TREVOR'S tutor in middle school. Truth be told, I didn't really help him with his studies; not to any measurable degree. We usually spent the 45 minute period, twice a week semi-flirting. I wasn't overly attracted to him (I was 12 years old for God's sakes), but my youthful ego liked the attention. I tried to help him with his reading, but we were routinely distracted. Fast forward several years to my junior year in high school. I had just returned from summer break and had finally "recovered" from my episode with anorexia nervosa. Due to my illness, my close knit friendships with my lifelong girlfriends had dissolved. I entered junior year feeling like a fish out of water. Without the support of my familiar peer group, I felt alone and scared. Trevor saw me in the hall one day and started in on his normal patterns of flirtation. I was in such a vulnerable space that I gobbled his attention right up. Trevor was charming and adorning. He had a way of making me feel like the only person in the world. This very trait is what ended up isolating me into becoming indeed pretty much the only person in his world, and more dangerously, him in mine.

As months passed, I slept with Trevor. I fell into what one could only call, young love. I didn't understand the chemical cocktail that was being released through the oxytocin surge that comes with being sexual active combined with the endocrine whirlwind that is being a pubescent girl. Dear God, it was a recipe for disaster. Long story short, I fell down the rabbit hole with Trevor. His friends became mine. His habits became mine. His hobbies became mine. The problem was his friends were druggies. His habits were to skip school and go to parties. His hobbies were to drink and do drugs. I was so young that I hadn't found myself yet and I had already managed to lose myself in a slurry of horrible choices and infatuation misunderstood by myself to be love. All of my choices were governed by desire. A desire to be loved. A desire to be accepted. A desire to normalize what had already been a testing and isolating high school career. Over the course of several years, Trevor and I rode an emotional roller-coaster. We'd get high and act intensely in love. He'd get wasted and become jealous and controlling. I'd shrink and contort how I was actually feeling into the portrayal of feelings that would slap a bandaid over the conflict as quickly as possible. We'd make up. We'd leap yet again into a period of extreme affection, just to fight again. The cycle was disease ridden, and I was too ignorant to acknowledge it. For three years I played in fire, and for three years I got burned. But make no mistake about it, it was not Trevor's fault. Trevor didn't force me into being lured by his flirtation that first day of junior year. He didn't force me to give him my virginity. Trevor didn't make me hang out with his friends, do drugs, fight, or make-up. We co-conspired that experience. And while the story sounds alarming, to this day I don't think Trevor had a malicious bone in his body. I don't think he ever meant to hurt me or bring me down. Trevor was simply as lost and misguided as I was. I mistakenly thought he could be my compass when his needle was spinning with zero direction. I can see clearly now that Trevor was my teacher.

IGNORANCE IS FUELED BY ALLOWING OUR CHOICES TO BE GOVERNED BY DESIRE AND NAIVETY. THE EFFECTS OF THESE CHOICES CAN BE DAMAGING, BUT IN A STATE OF IGNORANCE WE MISTAKE PAIN FOR PLEASURE.

Trevor taught me that if I make a decision to entangle my life with the life of someone else, I must first establish a firm ability to stand on my own two feet. Two people stumbling along together, both with wobbly legs simply won't make it very far. He taught me that recognizing someone's big heart and enjoying their ability to make you feel better about yourself are not necessarily grounds for a relationship. With Trevor I had the opportunity to be young and ignorant and make massive mistakes. Thank God, for the divine presence that kept me alive and out of prison during the tumultuous learning period.

Truth:

Ignorance in Sanskrit, the language of *The Yoga Sutras*, is Avidya. It functions off a lack of awareness and understanding of truth. Ignorance is fueled by allowing our choices to be governed by desire and naivety. The effects of these choices can be damaging, but in a state of ignorance we mistake pain for pleasure. In essence, in a state of ignorance, we're playing with fire, completely oblivious to how bad we're being burned.

Practice:

Become distinctly aware of the effects of your choices. How do you feel when you choose A? How do you feel when you chose B? Really go inward and examine your emotional state after each choice. Did option A give you a sense of momentary elation that shortly thereafter plummeted into a feeling of regret or exhaustion? Did option B feel less adrenaline charged, but gave you a sustained feeling of satisfaction and peace? During the process of cultivating awareness take care not to place guilt or shame over your experience. Whatever you chose, it served its purpose because it gave you an opportunity to learn. But the aim in examining the effects of our choices is to become crystal clear about what choices cause us pain and what choices create peace. We want to overcome ignorance so that good choices become reflexive and habitual.

DVESHA : AVERSION

My College Boyfriend: Gram

Story:

GRAM AND I went to the same high school, but we didn't know each other then. We met more materially when I came home from college during winter break of my sophomore year. I was waitressing at a local restaurant to earn extra cash. He and some friends came in. I was their server. He had strong arms, sun kissed blonde hair, and carried himself with a maturity that felt new to me. By this stage in my life, I had moved past my curiosity for and entrapment with drugs and partying. I wasn't really interested in drinking either. I had firmly switched gears from being party girl into being a studious homebody. I was more interested in ruminating through my mind while taking long walks on the beach, and watching documentaries about the food industry and the environment than anything else. Gram had just graduated from college and had just moved home to begin looking for a job. He wanted to establish his career in commercial real estate. I was already planning to transfer to a new university at the onset of the new semester. We started dating just a few weeks before Christmas, so there were ample opportunities to partake in holiday festivities. I joined Gram for several nights out. Our connection was natural and our banter always stimulating. He played into my newly discovered intellectual and spiritual side. He introduced me to books such as *The Power of Now and Conversations with God*. Gram meditated, played the guitar (granted, not very well), and seemed entrepreneurial. He hooked me with the faculties of his mind. We had a more substantial relationship than I had known with previous partners. We talked about spirituality, politics, the inner dynamics of our families, how we overcame tough times, health, and even business strategies. We went out to eat, to movies, bowling, and on walks. We enjoyed a healthy lifestyle together. We fell into a stable and predictable routine, and only occasionally shared a glass of red wine. We were both enjoying our connection and the simplicity of life. For several months everything was great.

Then tragically, Gram's brother, a couple years his junior, was killed in a motorcycle accident. I didn't realize it then, but that's when things shifted. The devastation and stress of losing his brother caused Gram's lifelong back and hip pain to flare up. He started taking the pain killers he had been prescribed for decades, but rarely touched. Gradually, he increased his dosage. He started abusing the medicine and became addicted to prescription drugs. Gram was avoiding pain in the most convenient way he knew. Some nights I would come home from a long day at school and a busy shift at the restaurant and stretch in bed. He could sense that my body was sore and inflamed. He offered me pain killers. Repeatedly, I declined. But one night I finally said yes. I took the painkiller. My body felt like it was melting. My skin was sweetly sensitive to touch. I felt warm, tingly, and shamelessness good in the beginning. My use started out as sporadic, but sadly became a habit. I too had fallen into the trap of actively escaping my pain. Unknowingly, I was actually actively avoiding my own growth and fulfillment. I had become a robot that woke up, took a painkiller, moved through the day with a distorted perception (a dance of being high and numb) and went to sleep. Repeat. Unintentionally. Mindlessly we had crafted an existence where we cheated our way into a comfort zone of monotony. We foolishly thought pain would never find us. The very thing that dissolved pain had over time become the source of pain. I felt endlessly guilty taking pills. While they came in a medicinal bottle and were prescribed by a physician (granted, not to me), I couldn't justify it to myself any longer. I was doing drugs again. And because painkillers turn off our receptors for pain, and everything in the universe functions on a scale of balance, the pills had also turned off my receptors for joy. I felt guilt and malaise. I couldn't take it anymore. I took myself off the pills. Shortly after, Gram did too; momentarily at least. The withdrawals were intense. I shivered while dripping in clammy sweat. I broke out in acne, felt irritable, and had a bout of depression. Thankfully, once the medication was out of my system a flow of fresh energy surged through me. I graduated from school, and with a new wave of vitality, I decided to go on a solo backpacking trip through Europe. Gram at that point was busy with his new career and wouldn't be joining me.

I had an eye opening and amazing three month adventure. I returned at the height of the economic crisis. My relationship with Gram had fizzled drastically. Unable to find a substantial job, I recalled stories friends I made while backpacking shared about how they loved teaching English in Asia. I decided to apply for a job as an English teacher at English College in China. I got it. Within weeks I ended my relationship as I knew it with Gram and packed my bags for Asia. I wasn't numb anymore. I was the opposite. I was tingly with excitement. And I wasn't scared of pain anymore. I was ready to feel all life had to offer; knowing there would be a cornucopia of days of happiness, and yes, there would be days of pain. I was more than okay with that.

Gram too, was my teacher. I have boundless gratitude for Gram because he introduced me to spiritual books, one author in particular, Wayne Dyer, who became my venerable teacher and through his craft, my mentor. Before Gram, I didn't enjoy reading. Through his suggestions, I feel in love with reading and owe the hundreds of books I've read in the time since to that catalytic period with him. Gram taught me that a reliable person and a structured schedule helped me feel safe in this world. He also taught me through the pernicious use of prescription medications, that I didn't need them. I didn't want them. And would never abuse them again. Gram taught me through our experience together that numbing pain does not eradicate pain. It just makes us less aware of it. That period of my life taught me that I want to be fully aware of the sources of both pain and to a heightened degree, the sources of happiness.

IN TRUTH, MANY PAINFUL EXPERIENCES SERVE THE ESTEEMED PURPOSE OF HELPING US GROW.

Truth:

Aversion, or Dvesha in Sanskrit is as it sounds, the avoidance of something; markedly pain. When we are pushed out of our comfort zones, we're faced head-on with a slew of emotions that are initially uncomfortable, or painful. The ego mind will tell us that something that feels pleasurable is good and something that feels uncomfortable or painful is bad. The ego does this to keep us trapped into a cycle of chasing desires. In truth, many painful experiences serve the esteemed purpose of helping us grow. Constantly avoiding pain is much like constantly avoiding growth. Numbing ourselves to placate the cry of aversion is one of the causes of suffering. We have to let ourselves feel.

Practice:

Aversion takes strong hold in our life through our habits. If we're motivated by the desire to avoid that which makes us uncomfortable, we will create for ourselves habits that keep us in our comfort zones. One way to move past aversion is to push yourself beyond your comfort zone. What is one thing you've been wanting to do, but you're scared. Don't think. Just answer. Good. Now, write it down. Look at that piece of paper and acknowledge all the excuses you've created for yourself to justify why you haven't done it yet. That thing that we've been wanting to do, and we all have one; the thing that has been waiting on a shelf for months, years, or decades now. That's the thing that will unshackle us from the bondage of aversion.

RAGA: ATTACHMENT

Bobby

Story:

I HAD JUST returned for six months in India. Yoga was my life and reason for existence. I woke up to practice yoga, rested, ate, read, practiced yoga again; rested, ate, read, and practiced again in the evening. Okay, it was a bit much, but at the time it was nourishing my soul. I felt emotionally lighter, more peaceful, and content than I ever had in my whole life. Upon returning to Florida from Asia, I moved back in with my parents. I needed to acclimate to the States, and figure out my career path. I was introduced to a yoga studio not far from my parent's house. The owner was a popular and well respected teacher. Her classes were buzzing with energy. I had previously only practiced yoga in Asia, so practicing in America opened my eyes to the dynamic production of the experience. Atmospheric lighting, music in surround, playful arm-balances, and much fancier poses than I had seen in Asia. I was enamored. One day I was tucked in the corner of a crowded vinyasa flow class. I was in my own little universe; practicing mostly with my eyes closed. But in wheel pose, which is a large backbend I opened my eyes, glanced across the room, and made prolonged eye contact with a very attractive yogi. He was toned and tan. He had big blue doughy eyes, and that kind of dewy thick skin that will never wrinkle. I'm not exaggerating when I say, there was an electric spark. (Okay, maybe it was my spine screaming to get out of the backbend.) Either way, that's how I met Bobby. After class he was sitting on the bench outside the studio. I can't say for certain, but it seemed like he was lingering, waiting to talk with me. We struck up a conversation—to no surprise about yoga and travel. An intuitive connection made itself known right off the bat, and it was clear we had a lot in common. We had both planted ourselves smack dab in the center of this yoga bubble. Our relationship moved at a light speed and a snail's pace at the same time. Having just returned from six months in India, I was enmeshed in the teachings of Indian Masters and modern day mystics, like Ram Dass and Bhagavad Dass. I wouldn't expect you to know or care who these people are. I didn't know anyone else stateside who knew or cared about anything I was living at the time. But Bobby and I were on the same philosophical wavelength. Knowing him instantly took my loneliness away. Our chemistry was out of this world. I repeatedly thought, I've known him, maybe in another life. He feels so familiar. What slowed our relationship down to the pace of a tranquilized sloth was Bobby's fear of relationships. He hadn't been in many serious relationships. He had never lived with a woman. He was an old soul, but in many respects, still largely immature. Granted he was 22 at the time; myself being just two years older. We spent the first year or so being hot and heavy, then he would retract for a few weeks, and we'd resist things again. Over a year into this on-and-off again friendship-based romance, we gained momentum and made our relationship official. We went to India together for five weeks. We explored the culture we had both subscribed to so heavily. But even there in India, I recall thinking, "He's hesitant. Part of him is not fully here with me, in the same emotional way that I'm here with him." We returned and moved into a little condo together. We both taught yoga full time, connected on every level, and took international trips together. The thing was, I always had this feeling that something was missing. Come to find out, Bobby's fear of commitment had incited him to drift into territories of infidelity several times throughout the course of our relationship. With each discovery of his chatting of sorts, my intuition that, "something is missing" was validated. What was missing was his complete loyalty and honesty. I can safely say the most sharp emotional pain I've ever experienced was when I learned Bobby cheated on me. I was so young, so innocent, and so in love. I can still recall the moment I found out he was disloyal. I remember not being able to take a breath. My chest collapsed into a literal stabbing somatic response. I called my best friend and she said something I'll never forget, "Breathe. You're okay. This is the worst it's going to feel. You'll never feel this bad again. You're okay. The worst is over." I suppose this sentiment brought me relief because I knew I was alive. If I had survived what I chose to believe the worst of it, I could survive anything. We were all young. The words might have not been as sage as I took them; but it didn't matter. The intention of bringing relief was both offered and received.

The story with Bobby didn't end with the uncovering of infidelity and the overcoming of the grief it caused. I returned. I chalked his wanderings up to being young and scared. I forgave him. "Forgive, but never forget," isn't that the phrase? Attachment with Bobby surfaced in two ways: 1. I became attached to the pain I experienced as a consequence of his actions. I routinely brought it up in conversation with him. His mistake and my pain loomed in the background of our relationship even as we moved forward. I attached to the story; therein variations of the same story repeated, and the relationship was constrained from blossoming. Our story was attached to pain because I attached the deeply personal pain I experienced to Bobby. Bobby was the trigger of that pain. He was not the source. The source of our pain is intimately and uniquely ours. Attaching the way we feel to anyone outside ourselves is a false attachment. I didn't know that then. And 2. I continued to return to Bobby for years, many years, seven or so, between other short term and long term boyfriends. I was attached to the comfort and familiarity that Bobby provided to me. I was attached to the idea that if that night I found out Bobby was unfaithful was the worst I would ever feel, then now Bobby is safe. He can never make me feel worse than that. I attached knowing I could handle pain to the believing I would always be safe. I can see clearly now that Bobby taught me that the soul's recognition of the soul of another is an intoxicating and sacred gift. But I also learned that we do not need to attach any additional enigmatic story to such a rare treat. It can be what it is, when it is, and if the course changes we do not have to attach ourselves to a story that it needs to be everlasting in the form in which it came. While my relationship with Bobby did and still does feel divine on some level, I've learned all relationships are divine. I believe nothing is based on happenstance, and if it is, the chance happening too can be sacred. Bobby taught me that I can feel at home simply by being in the presence of another human being. He also taught me that when that home is rearranged I can create a home in a new space; and doing so does not discredit the sweet abode that once housed my heart. Hearts are nomadic.

OUR SOUL IS THE ONLY THING THAT TRAVELS WITH US.

Truth:

Swami Vivekananda said, "All pain and misery come from attachment." The Vedas teach us that attachment is a source of human suffering because it causes us to cling and become possessive over people, relationships, material goods, and goals. The Buddha said, "You can only lose what you cling to." Yoda said, "Attachment leads to jealousy. The shadow of greed that is. Train yourself to let go of everything you fear to lose." Attachment can take many forms. In a state of attachment, we can mistake the memory of comfort and love we once had with someone for comfort and love that still exists, even though the comfort and love has morphed and is no longer ours to cling to. Gripping to something that is no longer there creates suffering. Being in a state of attachment could be striving for a goal that was once a healthy pursuit, but has changed course and should be set free. When life changes course, we should adapt with it. In the adaptation new goals will be revealed to us. Goals that align with our purpose. Goals that are fulfilling. Attaching to an aspiration which is no longer intended for us is like running a marathon and never finding the finish line. This kind of attachment is exhausting. Attaching ourselves to material goods such as our nice car, big house, or materially, youthful body is destined to bring pain because things are temporary. Attaching our identity and self-worth to material objects and the material body is bound to result in disappointment. We are invariably going to lose these elements. Our soul is the only thing that travels with us. Bringing our awareness and efforts to the functions of the soul, on the other hand will provide for us bountiful wellness and happiness. Spiritual teacher Sri Sri Ravi Shankar said, "Your non attachment to the mundane is your charm. Your attachment to the divine is your beauty." When we attach ourselves to things and the things inevitable disappear, we feel a sense of loss. Repeated loss can make us feel empty. When we identify with the infinite, with love and with the divine, we are then nearest to elements of existence that will never disappear. The proximity to the real is what fills us up! Yasmin Mogahed writes, "Try not to confuse 'attachment' with 'love', attachment is based on fear and dependency, and has more to do with love of self, than love of another. Love without attachment is the purest love because it isn't about what others can give you because you're empty. It is about what you can give to others because you're already full."

Practice:

Here, we're using a mantra to help rewire some of the outdated mental grooves, or neurological processes that have us stuck in patterns of holding on to things (or people) that no longer contribute to our lives and wellbeing. Our brains and thought processes are mailable. Mantras help us shape our perspective, and point the needle towards thoughts that lead to beliefs and experiences that are ultimately fulfilling. This is our mantra: "I am practicing non-attachment. I accept people and experiences as they come. I yolk wisdom and growth from my choices, and I allow people and experiences transform as life unfolds. I will not struggle or suffer to salvage anything that is no longer intended for me. I will express gratitude and release it as my Self sees fit. I trust the flow of life and understand that what is intended for me will be for me effortlessly."

Attachment: Build-Out

To take a brief pause from the Kleshas, or causes of suffering as described in the Vedic texts, I thought this would be a fitting place to include another perspective of the theme of attachment. This theory speaks to the way we navigate relationships based on our predisposition towards certain tendencies. As described in, *Attached*, written by Dr. Admit Levine and Rachel Heller, there are three basic attachment styles. While there can be fluidity in which style we most obviously identify with, typically each of us resonates strongly with one of these three styles:

1. **Anxious**
2. **Avoidant**
3. **Secure**

The anxious type drowns in an inordinate amount of energy. They routinely worry if their partner loves them. Anxious types feel a undeniable pull to spend a lot of time with their partner. They want their partner to be accessible and responsive. If their partner backs away, they panic.

The avoidant attachment style is nearly the opposite. People who have an avoidant attachment style value their independence more than relationships. These people are typically not the first to talk about their emotions or feel uncomfortable doing so. They're more prone to assigning blame when things are imbalanced versus re-aligning through a vulnerable discussion, or a discussion where they assume responsibility for the turbulence. These people tend to always be on the hunt for the "right" one. Which means they can easily write of someone who triggers them. They'll likely just say, "That person isn't right for me." Finally, we have the secure attachment style. These people are the cream of the crop in many ways. They strike a balance between caring, without worrying, and being both independent and intimate. They're happy to share feelings, collaborate, and compromise to maintain a harmonious relationship. A secure partner is a good indicator that the relationship will be successful. I found this system of categorization to be fascinating and helpful. It's useful to know that anxious and avoidant types are often attracted to one another, but these relationships are up against the odds because neither one will have their needs fulfilled. In fact, they feed into one another triggers. In retrospect, I can see this is the dynamic Bobby and I shared. I was the anxious type; constantly hungry for validation and more and more love. I desired intimate conversation and affection because I needed proof of our love reinforced. Bobby on the other hand felt uncomfortable talking about his emotions. Unknowingly at the time, my need for closeness pushed him further way. Vulnerability frightened him. As an avoidant type, it was more natural for Bobby to emotionally distance himself from me and create space by cheating. Even when we discussed the instance years after the fact he said, "I loved you. I just didn't know if we were right for each other." Listen, we can't put ourselves or people into boxes. We're all nuanced and changeable creatures, however based on this psychological theory, we do have a proclivity to navigate relationships in accordance to the qualities assigned to one of these three styles.

Dr. Levine makes the argument that secure types are most desirable in that being a secure type or with a secure type is the best predictor of a happy relationship. With this being said, I delved into, 'How do we become people who navigate relationships with a secure attachment style?' Again, people with secure attachment styles are honest, communicative, authentic, emotionally available, confident in who they are, patient, and willing to compromise. Secure people are as they sound, solid. So how do we lean into being secure through this lens? The answer mimics the core theme of this book… for the composition of someone who processes and embodies self-love is that of a secure person. Someone who has invested in self-awareness, is aware of their fears—yet thinks and acts in a way that is far elevated above the level of fear, and is unshakable in their own skin…that is self-love and that is "secure". As hindsight tends to offer us a more clear of view, it's easy to see now that nearly all of my relationships were based on the archetypal interplay of the anxious and avoidant. It's simple to draw a parallels between Raga, the Vedic term and conditions that describe the attachment that causes suffering and the anxious attachment style. To highlight, the Buddha said, "You can only lose what you cling to." In my personal experience in dating in my twenties, I set myself up for suffering. I was constantly clinging to something, which meant I was inevitably going to lose something the moment my grip slipped. We've established now that self-love is sustainable because once it is established it cannot be taken away. Okay, now we will return to the Vedas and the next Klesha, or cause of suffering…and the next relationship. Meet Mett.

Mett

Story:

METT HAD A glowing resume. A gifted engineer, best selling author, and a talented musician. He was the only person I've ever personally known who had a wikipedia page. I wasn't initially attracted to Mett. We were friends, but the sparkle of his out of the box thinking, expansive world view, and remarkable creativity lured me in. Mett came from a well known, affluent family. Everyone in his family appealed to me. His sister, a gorgeous vocalist, his father, a spiritual teacher, and his mother a devoted goddess of a Hindu spiritual path, called Bhakti. They lived in lavish homes with marble floors that sparkled in grandeur. Materially, they seemed the to be the epitome of success. And spiritually, so magnetically enlightened.

I entered my relationship with Mett at the level of intrigue. I had no agenda or intention to propel my advancement, or status through him. With Mett, my mind just seemed prone towards boundless wonder. We united in the realms of wanting to learn about health, and humanity. And wanting to create beauty through music, movement, and art. Mett showed me a new world by bringing me to summit conventions with proving thought-leaders, political fundraisers, fancy dinner parties, and The Grammys. But introducing me to these experiences was like dressing a baby in Louis Vuitton. I was unfazed by the social positioning, but transfixed by the way the rich textures felt against my skin. The first year of our relationship was one of novelty and an amplified sense of how big the world is, and how special I could be within it. In contrast to this, my relationship with Mett was simultaneously littered with insecurity. I felt a permeating sense of unworthiness, as though I wasn't smart enough, glamorous enough, or sophisticated enough to fit into his world. Our journey together was riddled with landmines where the world views and experiences he introduced me to routinely triggered my deepest fears of not belonging and not being good enough. At our peak together, we created a Cirque Du Soleil style show that blended my aptitude for yoga and his musical capabilities. We worked in partnership to recruit dancers, ariel artists, musicians, and various performers to create sold out performances. The entire process was a collaborative labor of love; long hours of late night choreography, rehearsals, and planning. Then just a couple months before opening night, Mett was working on the graphics for promotional material and much to my shock and dismay he slapped his name over the title of our show. All of a sudden a large piece of the joy I found in our collaborative project was swallowed up by what felt like an assault from the powerful hand of a roaring ego. In fairness, when I approached him about how unsettled I was in the way he plastered HIS name over OUR creation, he claimed it was a business decision. As though one day he'd sell the rights to our show, and attach our little show to some sort of larger enterprise. I shrank. It all felt dirty to me. His ego's need to plaster his name on our show, blew my ego's desire to be equally validated. I didn't argue my case. I retreated quietly into my familiar territory of avoiding confrontation, but with it some of my enthusiasm and confidence retreated as well. Our show was created from a space that was aligned with purpose and fulfillment. Our mission was simply to spread beauty and inspiration. In retrospect, I realize what tripped us up. When the representation of the soul becomes the driving animator of our life, the ego gets really friggin' scared. The ego knows that the recognition of the souls function through a human life is invariably the imminent extinction of the ego. In one last ditch effort, the ego tries to salvage what little authority it has over the soul by becoming garishly demanding. Mett and I had created something that exemplified our souls, and the ego simply wasn't having it. I didn't think then, and I don't think now that Mett had or has a raging ego. I think his ego just behaved as any ego would in a threatened state. It became bloated and inflamed. It fought for its survival. In this case, it won. An experience that could have been an operation of pure soul was interrupted by the egos need to label and claim credit. Mett escorted me into a world of broadened horizons, with open access to glamour and prestige. He crafted for himself a world that seemed limitless, and at the effect of sharing time together I shattered many of my own self-limiting glass ceilings. Mett was a visionary in his ability to create and shape people's perception of him, which is undoubtedly why before we even started dating I placed him on a pedestal of being a brilliant engineer and creative genius. I'm undecided if it was the fulfillment of his soul or the determination of his ego that enabled him to mold illusions into reality. What I do know is that when the recognition of the soul is dormant, the ego's job is easy. The ego doesn't have to fight for power if the soul isn't engaged. But when we awaken to the souls ability to conduct our life, we must be vigilant to the manipulative tactics of the ego. My experience with Mett made clear to me that it is when the soul is shining that the ego becomes even more scandalous. But Mett also taught me that the human experience can be an experience of creativity, wonder, and awe. He reminded me of my ability to be masterful creator.

Truth:

The ego is obsessed with labels. It uses labels as a device to delineate the world and its inhabitants. Labels keep us confined, little, and ceaselessly hungry for the shinier version of the latest upgraded label.

THE EGO KNOWS THAT THE RECOGNITION OF THE SOULS FUNCTION THROUGH A HUMAN LIFE IS INVARIABLY THE IMMINENT EXTINCTION OF THE EGO.

The ego is too small minded to understand the interconnectedness of existence; that we all play a valuable role that contributes to the ongoing advancement of the greater whole. The ego can't fathom a world where everyone is equal, because it's greatest thrill is making one better than, and consequently, another less than. The ego uses designations of status and hierarchy to attempt to keep us separate. In this separation, the ego is destined to loneliness, thereby seeking company through the recruitment of propagating its lies. The lies look something like this: You'll be happy when (fill in the blank). The attainment of this house (car/boat/partner/business deal…) will earn you the respect you've been craving. A bloated bank account will declare your worth. Fame and recognition will give your life meaning. The slogans of the ego are perilous bottomless pits. Make no mistake about it —the demands of the ego are never going to be satisfied. The ego aims for achievement. The higher Self aims for fulfillment. Fulfillment is the result of creating and contributing at the level of soul. Fulfillment is not attached to recognition, accolades, and material gain. Fulfillment is the elevated version of achievement. It is built on the grounds of purpose and humility. And as we approach nearer and nearer to fulfillment through the recognition of our souls purpose and employment of our God-given talents, the ego will get louder and louder in attempts to claim credit and rob us of supreme satisfaction that is intrinsic to work produced by pure soul.

Practice:

Intentions serve as safe touch point to the soul. And we recall staying close to the soul keeps the ego at bay. Goals on the other hand can be result driven and can easily lead us towards egocentric behaviors. Where goals are associated with results; intentions are connected to processes.

FULFILLMENT IS THE ELEVATED VERSION OF ACHIEVEMENT. IT IS BUILT ON THE GROUNDS OF PURPOSE AND HUMILITY.

A goal is typically more tangible and absolute, such as I will increase my business revenue by 20 percent this year, or I will lose five pounds this month, or I will earn my GPA this semester. Goals are quantifiable. Intentions happen on the quantum level. Intentions may not be seen, but they are felt and experienced. If my aim is to increase my business revenue this year; rather than setting a goal which can be seen as a success or failure depending on the outcome; I can set the intention of, "I am abundant" because indeed the effect of increasing my revenue, the way I desire to feel is abundant. The number is actually less relevant. It's the feeling I'm aiming for. Through an intention there can be no quote-unquote success or failure. There can only be a captivating sense of process. Intentions are sweet and effective pipelines towards advancing our paths with the accompaniment of soul. I prefer to set my intentions in the I AM format. Intentions stating in the present have greater strength than intentions that are set in the future. Intentions phrased in the future tense feel more like wishful thinking, whereas intentions stated in the present tense feel like solid truths.

CLINGING TO LIFE

James

Story:

JAMES AND I were introduced right off the tails of my break up with Mett. We were put together to model for an 'athleisure' fashion show, which is comical by the way because neither of us are models. Basically, the event planners just needed a couple of tallish people who were willing to wear fancy athletic gear and smile for the camera. Upon meeting James, my first impression was that he was a ladies man. He was charming and was schmoozing up the real models like there was no tomorrow. In retrospect, the ironic part about this is we were both approaching life like there was indeed no tomorrow. I was in my early thirties, had just invested a couple years and a ton of energy into a relationship that came to a screeching halt. My biological clock was ticking away. My dreams of ever wearing a white dress was slipping away. And I could not seem to do anything fast enough. On James' side of the coin, he was obsessed with his career. His career was his outlet for his raging ambition, material gain, and to an astounding degree—his sense of self-worth and value. I was clinging to my left ring finger and ovaries for dear life, and he was clinging to his career with all his might. Neither of us consciously realized this then by the way. Not at the level that hindsight has so generously revealed anyway. What I was aware of at the time though was that I could not in good faith just jump into another relationship. Mett mattered to me. Losing him required a processing period, and more substantially still, coming to terms that the dream for a creating a family any time soon simply wasn't in my present cards. As James pursued me, I was interested, but knew I wasn't ready. I asked him to give me time to decompress. I later learned he assumed I needed downtime because of work exhaustion or something. No, that's what he probably needed. What I needed was time to put my heart back together. After several months, we began dating. Our first date turned quite literally into eighteen months. James and I had an instant connection. Within weeks, I was practically living at his place and within months, we were house shopping. It's almost comedic to write this now, because from this vantage point the red flags are pretty much flapping in my face. We were both clinging to a life that didn't even materially exist yet. In time, James' compulsion to work insane hours and leap ahead in his career took a toll on our relationship. Our playful two peas in a pod dynamic morphed into two stress balls passing in the night. James stressed due to inhumane hours of sleep and self-care. My stress was mostly accentuated by the haunting trajectory of our relationship. Two people growing apart should not move towards marriage, and surely not towards starting a family. But logic is useless and mostly invisible to an emotional creature fixated on a clock that seemed to be ticking down more rapidly by the hour. See here, James and I were clinging to life. Both of our minds hijacked by fear. The irony is by clinging to a life that wasn't naturally in harmony with where we were, we were missing the potentially fabulous life that was right in front of our eyes. Long story short, James got a new job in a new city. Under the stipulation that an engagement was promised for a few months after the move, I moved too. A few months later the fragility of our relationship conceded to the cracks and we went our separate ways. I'm grateful to James because he taught me never to swap the holistic experience of a joyful life for the one pointed experience of achieving a particular goal in accordance to one particular measure of time. The truth is, James and I were meant to be short term teachers for each other. We weren't meant to get married and start a family. How do I know this? Because we didn't. And if we were intended to do that in this life we would have. But I do know that if we would have stepped back and appreciated the life we had together instead of beelining our way to the next destination point we could have found more joy and peace in the process.

The truth is clinging to life is basically resisting death. And being scared of death can cause us to swap being truly alive for simply living, or worse yet, just making a living. I can see clearly now that

I was responsible for my own suffering with James because I was clinging to a life with a person that I wasn't truly compatible with because I was fearful that my life would slip away before I became a wife and a mother. I know for certain now that story was entirely based on fear; not reality. In reality, a number does not determine my vitality and I am worthy of being in a relationship based on mutual respect and aspirations. Clinging to something painful will not bring pleasure. But releasing something painful will indeed create space for pleasure.

Truth:

Patanjali Yoga Sutras illustrates the final cause of suffering as fear, more specifically, the clinging to life, even a life of misery because one is fearful of death. The fear of death causes one to identify with an inaccurate sense of self and the physical world. When someone is tangled in the bondage of this affliction they unknowingly tighten their bondage by wrapping themselves in the items they incorrectly perceive as the items that compose a life. When we're scared of dying we can adorn ourselves in material items such as a sculpted body, a high-rise condo, or a high profile job as though these items will offer us survival insurance. But what the fearful person does not realize is that focusing on the material and temporary conditions that can control does not lead to immortality. When we're scared of dying we can also try to manufacture picture perfect concepts of what we falsely identify as truly living. For me, this meant forcing a relationship that could grow into me becoming a mother, however miserable the relationship was, all because I was terrified of dying before I fulfilled that role. Obsessing over attaining anything, rather it be a larger paycheck or parenthood is not living. It's life sucking. It's fear. Attaining a certain status or role will never exempt us from the inevitable. No one is exempt from death. Spending our lives trying to earn a superpower that isn't in the design of the universe can cause us to turn our backs on our own precious life. The irony is, we can, and many of us do, almost kill ourselves trying to earn a superhero cape that can help us fly over fear. Sadly, it is the cape that strangles us. The way to overcome the fear of death is to focus not on earning a living, but on creating a life; a true, honest, authentic life that is adorned not in finite things, but infinite qualities. Qualities that create moments of laughter, play, snuggles, and tears where pain surrenders because of heart penetrating connections. These are the moments worth living.

To shift from the fear of dying to actually living we must correctly identify what elements compose a rich and worthwhile life. The ingredients for a life worth living can not be manufactured. If you place your hands over your chest you will feel your heartbeat. This heart beat is a reminder you have vitality coursing through your veins. Perhaps you did not choose this heart beat, but it chose you. You are here and you are living for a reason. This life is a gift and using it to fabricate reasons to prove we exist versus actually existing is not only wasteful; it induces suffering.

Practice:

This exercise is literally exercise. Go do a dozen jumping jacks, sprint down your street and back, jump off the diving board, or turn on your favorite song and dance around your living room. Feel your heart pulsating in your chest. Feel the rush that comes with warm blood and sensitive nerve endings.

Feel the glow on your skin and the luminosity in your eyes. Feel what it feels like to be truly alive. Appreciate it. And then take a deep breath in and a huge sigh out. Release all the air. Again slow deep breath in and slow full and complete breath out. Press all the air out of both lungs until your lungs are fully empty. Feel the natural craving for a new breath; then go ahead and sip it in. The Buddhist believe that each exhale represents a miniature death and each inhale represents a rebirth. By watching our breath for a few cycles we metaphorically have the experience of dying and being reborn. Watching the breath teaches us about the natural ebbs and flows of life. It reminds us that coming and going is a natural response to life. Our breath reminds us that life is about surrendering (exhaling) to create space for the new (inhaling). Enjoy your breath.

Okay, I'm with you. That might have sounded like a laundry list of failures. But this is not so. Not to go all Tony Robbins on you, but what looks like a failure at first glance was actually an epic opportunity to grow and move forward with if nothing else, a bit more wisdom. I have an adage that I believe I made up because I can't recall where it came from, "Your past can either be your baggage or your wisdom. Your choice." I choose wisdom. I choose to be grateful for each of these people. I choose to forgive myself for the mistakes I made. I choose to see the silver linings in all circumstances. It is nearly in the definition of being a seeker to always be seeking the pearls of wisdom that enhance the human experience. Relationships, for however long they last, give us madhouse mirrors reflecting back to us both the belief systems that serve us, and the ones that don't, along with treasure chests full of wisdom should we so choose to partake. I recall the idiom, "Fail and fail fast, that's the key to success." The idea is that we don't learn from our successes, they can be celebrated for sure; we deserve those in abundance too, but as life functions in schemes of duality; we need the failures too. It is the failures that serve as catalysts for our shifts and layers of transformations.

CHAPTER FIFTEEN

The Four Agreements

Story:

FOLLOWING UP ON one of the last phrases in the previous chapter, "Fail and fail fast. That's the key to success," now I'm going to share an unconventional success story. Girl meets boy. Girl falls for boy. Boy falls for girl. They share an elevated week together. He returns to Philadelphia (he was only visiting girl's home city for work.) They share an enticing long distance romance for three weeks. He plans a return visit, complete with a snazzy hotel suite, champagne, and fluffy spa robes. Girl can't wait and is counting down the day for his return visit. Boy is sweetly sending charming countdown alerts as the visit nears closer…Yes, you guessed it. The girl was me, and the story that appears to be out of a Nicholas Sparks book is about to turn into a bust. But not so fast, this bust is the most enlightened and authentic turn around said "girl" has experienced in her life so far. Here's why: A. she was impeccable with her word. B. she didn't take anything personally. C. she didn't make assumptions, and D. she did her best. These are the laws of the Toltec tradition, or more popularly known as *The Four Agreements*.

Steve was all set to fly in Saturday just after noon. I had my morning planned. I'd go on a bike ride, teach my yoga class, eat lunch, shower and dress, meditate (to calm my overly enthused nerves), and head to the airport to pick up Steve. Going to bed Friday night, the plan seemed flawless. But Saturday morning was a different story. I woke up with anxiety, which while this was a common feeling years ago; it is an extremely rare occurrence now days. I took a few deep breaths upon rising with anxiety, drank a cup of tea, and set off for my bike ride. I presumed seeing the sun rise over the bay would put me at ease. Twilight turning to daylight did soothe me a little, but I still felt undercurrents of anxiety and disease. I got quiet and listened to my gut. I heard, *be still*. It didn't make complete sense at the moment, but I stored, *be still* in the back of my mind incase I needed it later. I went through the various steps of my morning and retrieved Steve from the airport. My anxiety accelerated. I recalled, *be still*. I knew then to just relax and find the stillness that was underneath my uneasiness. I knew I needed to give this a shot because I really liked Steve. I anticipated his arrival for weeks now and he was generous and kind to plan this visit. Plus, I didn't know the reason I was anxious. It could have very well been a separate root cause apart from his visit. Steve and I checked into the hotel and had a glass of wine at the hotel bar. We walked around the city and enjoyed the sunshine. We met friends for dinner and they joined us for bowling. Optically it seemed quintessential. Inside, I was still uneasy. That night my intuition blared through my body. My cycle kicked in with a vengeance. I hadn't been sick by means of vomiting in probably ten plus years. My body was shutting down. I spent the night in the bathroom alternating between crouching over the toilet and taking hot baths. I got maybe two hours of intermittent sleep. Steve slept like a rock. Thank goodness for that. In the morning, I obviously felt off, but I thought it might be due to lack of sleep. Here's where I applied the principles. I told Steve I wasn't feeling like myself and I needed some fresh air. I left the hotel, but told him I'd be back in a few hours. While I was clearing my head in nature I swallowed a big pill of honesty. First with myself. I more than realized, on a visceral level I knew Steve and I were not an energetic match. In the past I might have focused on the way he possesses all the qualities I respect in a man, and talked myself into making it work. I knew at the level of gut, it wasn't right. In the past I might have manipulated my internal narrative to avoid any type of conflict and certainly swallowed my tongue as to not make him feel uncomfortable or unfavorable towards me. I knew I could not. Not this time. It wouldn't have been fair to me and certainly not fair to Steve. He deserved to know the truth. He deserved my honesty. And we both deserved the advantage that comes with one being impeccable with their word. We both would benefit from my microscopic truth;

from me explaining exactly how I was feeling and what I was thinking without any added fluff of dramatic flare. Straightforward honesty. Clear and compassionate. That's what would suit us best. So I carried on. I returned to the hotel and opened up to Steve. It was vulnerable. It wasn't smooth. But it was authentic. And it was pure. Steve couldn't have been more considerate. He responded with, "Thank you for telling me. I know that wasn't easy for you to say. You are a good person. It's okay. Sometimes things just don't work out." Agreement number two: neither of us took it personally. We knew it wasn't a stab at either of our personalities or characters. We just weren't an ideal fit. Agreement number three: Don't make assumptions. I asked him how he was feeling. He expressed that he would digest it and move forward. His inaudible communication, body language and eye contact said he was hurt, but would be fine. I didn't assume he was complacent or crushed. I gave him the space to express himself to the degree he felt comfortable, just as he had done for me. And finally, the fourth agreement: do your best. The situation was not ideal. We planned a romantic reunion and instead we parted ways in less than 24 hours. I wasn't without my fumbles, and he was rightfully so, very distant as we said goodbye. But we did our best. With complete respect and kindness towards one another, we navigated a situation that could have been drawn out or ugly with our best attempt at precision and grace. We did our best. I'm aware that doesn't sound like a traditional success story, but for me it was a meaningful relationship that was handled with integrity from start to finish. It was the most evolved "break-up" I've had to date. This isn't a victory. It's evolution. Love takes many forms and the way I see it, when two people can sustain self-love and express themselves lovingly even in through tough circumstances; that's success.

Truth:

The Four Agreements are four concise truths based on the Toltec wisdom. Renowned author, Don Miguel Ruiz made *The Four Agreements* a global sensation with his best selling book designed to help us create love and happiness in our lives. The agreements are as simple as they are profound. I first stumbled upon this book in my early twenties, without fail, since then, anytime I face adversity and check in with the four agreements I have undeniably broken at least one of the four agreements and my breaking of the agreement is indeed what has contributed to my own discord. We'll use the next few chapters to break down The Four Agreements:

1. **Be Impeccable with your word.** This is to say, speak with integrity. Say only what you mean. Avoid using words that are derogatory or misleading to others or self-deprecating or limiting towards yourself. Use the power of the word in the direction of truth and love. In the book *Why You're Not Married Yet,* Tracy McMillan writes, "Men won't lie to you, but they'll let you lie to yourself." While I don't think this is gender specific, I think she's on to something. Humans are wired to avoid pain and seek pleasure. If we're wrapped in a pleasurable experience we generally want to stay there, even if that means overlooking elements of truth and transparency. Here's a real life example. (I've been an open book so far, why stop now?) I was dating a guy named Sean. Our dynamic was playful, affectionate, and relaxing. We mimicked nearly the same date on a once a week basis. He'd pick me up on Tuesday morning, we'd go out on the boat all

day, exploring islands and new little canals and inlets. We'd pop open a bottle of champagne, eat a nice meal, head home and shower, and cuddle while watching documentaries. It was in my mind, perfect. Then over a month in, it occurred to me that I only see Sean on Tuesdays. I knew he had a demanding work schedule and often worked overnight hours in medicine at the hospital. (yes, I too might be thinking what you're thinking at this point…Oh my word. He was married!) Luckily, no! However when I was prompted by the Four Agreements to not make assumptions, because until then I had presumed we were exclusive and not seeing other people based on our level of intimacy; I learned that for me McMillian was indeed onto something. "Men won't lie to you, but they'll let you lie to yourself." It was late one evening and I knew Sean was at work, but the anticipation to know if he was indeed treating our relationship as a committed one or not was overflowing within me. I texted him, "Can you call when you're free?" My phone rang right away. I decided not to dance around and just come right out and ask, "Are you seeing anyone else?" His response was something along the lines of, "Oh, if you want to see other people that's okay with me. I'm not a jealous person. I want you to be happy. But I do love spending time with you and I'm excited about getting to know you even more." That said it all. Without saying anything, really. Sean wasn't impeccable with his word. He smeared icing all over the cake. But baked into the cake was essentially, "Of course I'm seeing other people, but I don't want that small little fact to stop me from seeing you." Sean didn't lie. He simply wasn't impeccable with his word. You can guess how long that lasted.

2. **Don't take anything personally.** Nothing others do is because of you. What others say is a projection of their own reality, their own dream. When you are immune to the opinions and actions of others, you won't be the victim of needless suffering. Wayne Dyer says, "No one can offend you without your own consent." Tracy McMillan says, "People are not doing anything to you. They are just doing. You just happen to be in the vicinity." Going back to Sean. I knew not to take the reality that we were

on two different pages personally. Simply said, it wasn't personal.

3. **Don't make assumptions.** Find the courage to ask questions and to express what you really want. Communicate with others as clearly as you can to avoid misunderstandings, sadness, and drama. With just one agreement, you can completely transform your life. (See Agreement number one for anecdote).

4. **Always do your best.** Your best is going to change from moment to moment. It will be different from when you are a healthy person to when you are ill. Your best was different when you were in high school, than it is now. Doing our best is on an evolutionary spectrum. Maya Angelou said, "When people know better, they do better." With experience and awareness we know better, which means the measures in which we can do better are higher. For me the Four Agreements give a frame to architectural integrity. The four walls are held up by the Four Agreements; now how we choose to cover the walls is up to us.

Practice:

This practice has come in handy for me hundreds of times over the last ten years. It's basically just a check in check list. Any time you feel adversely to the situation at hand pause and ask yourself: Am I being impeccable with my word? Am I taking this personally? Am I making assumptions? Am I doing my best? Again, it's not so much about the finding a polished answer or solution; it's about noticing. Asking the question allows you to reframe the situation through an exalted perspective. *The Four Agreements* help us stay in integrity with our Self while nourishing a landscape where we can keep peace in any given situation. Personally, making assumptions is a big one for me. Keep an eye on that one. It can be insidious.

CHAPTER SIXTEEN

Forgiveness & Compassion

Story:

I'M USING AN entirely fictitious name here because who the person is is irrelevant. You'll recall from early on in our time together that we are not our stories. The sharing of this and all of these stories, are here to convey the moral. So, as the story goes it was a squelching hot July summer night. I was sitting at home perusing old photos on my phone. I stumbled upon an album of photos of "Bob" and I. Seeing us so happy together made me nostalgic. I hadn't spoken to Bob in nearly a year, but in a flash on spontaneity I decided to text him. I sent him one of our happy photos and said, "Hey there! I just stumbled upon this. How are you? Would love to catch up soon." Within minutes he replied back, asked what I was up to, and if I'd like to come over to go for a walk or something. I said sure and that I would be there shortly. It took me longer than expected to get dressed and head over. I arrived about an hour later. When I arrived I knocked on the door and heard the sound of a woman's voice behind the door. I obviously thought this was curious and didn't have the best feeling about it. A second later, the door opened. A woman was standing with her body hidden behind the door as she just peered her pretty face to the side to see who it was. It was me. Instantly, all of the blood drained from my face and my heart took on a whole new tempo. It was beating so fast in my chest. In a stumbling voice I said, "Ummm, is everything okay? I'm sorry. I thought I was meeting Bob. I'll go." I turned to walk away. I was mortified. The woman quickly and politely said, "No, no, please don't go. I need to talk to you. Please wait one second while I put clothes on. I'll be right out." *Dear God!* 30 seconds later, out she comes. "Hi, my name is Becky. I know who you are. You're Kristen. Not to be weird, but I've followed you on social media. You seem like a really nice person and Bob speaks highly of you." I was so confused. She proceeded, "Please sit. Can we talk for a second? I know you used to date Bob. Full disclosure, we broke up two weeks ago. Bob and I dated for about three months, but we're not anymore. I came over tonight unannounced and he was so short with me and kept telling me I need to leave. I understand why now. You were coming. Well obviously I stayed. I'm sorry. I didn't know you were coming. Anyway, the reason I came is because I've been worried about him. His depression has gotten really bad. I'm sure you dealt with it while you two were together too, correct?" Whoa, this was a lot to take in. I responded, "Yes, he had episodes while we were together." (I knew at this point that this situation was not my business and I needed to go). I carried on, "Becky, you seem very kind. Under different circumstances, I think you and I would be friends. However, there's nothing I can do. I empathize with your concern for Bob. The truth is however, that you nor I can help him if he doesn't want to help himself." My heart had slowed down. Sweat was dripping down my face. His new girlfriend of sorts looked fresh and gorgeous. I felt utterly zapped of energy. "Becky, I'm going to go now. I wish you the best." I leaned over and she leaned in. We hugged. She walked back in turning around to wave bye, and I drove home.

In the car I was both shocked and exhausted. That was not how I anticipated the night to unfold. But at the same moment I was grateful. Perhaps I needed a certain solidity in my closure with Bob. That definitely sealed the entrance to ever revisiting that relationship. When I got home I immediately took a shower. I felt dirty. Dirty in a number of ways. I knew I needed more than a shower. I needed to forgive myself for getting into such a stupid situation. I needed to recognize that A. I was lonely. B. I was vulnerable. C. I didn't have all the facts, and D. I was hopeful. None of these things were stupid. I was not stupid. I did not do anything wrong. I needed to remind myself that I was loved and loving. I stood still in the shower and as the refreshing water rinsed down my body, I recited my affirmations. I AM love. I AM Whole. I AM Complete. I knew based on experience how effective using affirmations had been for me. I knew that affirmations allow the storyline of fear to be stopped and redirected. As I dried off, I knelt down on my bathmat and released Bob. *Dear God*, I said, *I release Bob from my heart. My angels surround him and help him. I release him.* Then, I went to bed. I slept hard. When I woke up in the morning, Bob had texted several times apologizing and trying to explain and justify the cluster-fuck of a situation. I simply said, "No worries. I wish you well." and that was it.

Truth:

For me, forgiveness lives inside compassion. Compassion is offering one another grace and forgiveness. The type of forgiveness I'm referring to is not one of righteousness or moral superiority. Forgiveness isn't a hyperbolic, 'He screwed up because he's not emotionally evolved and I am, so I'll let him off the hook.' Forgiving someone is an act of generosity towards ourselves and the other party. It's saying, *I acknowledge you. I acknowledge what happened. I acknowledge we're human. And I love myself enough to not be continuously pained by something outside of myself.* Compassionate forgiveness rests in the core acknowledgment that at our core we are all humans.

We're all doing our best based on our current level of awareness. Compassionate forgiveness is the recognition of shared humanity with whoever stands before us. It is understanding the imminent errors laden in being human. Compassionate forgiveness is offered inwardly as it is outwardly. The paradox is in affording ourselves forgiveness and compassion when offering another forgiveness and compassion is challenging. In my experience, it's normal to feel some resistance in offering others grace. We have to hurdle over the magnetic plateau of our own fears before reaching an elevated state of grace. Even when it's hard, it's always worth the leap. A feature to becoming compassionately forgiving to me is in recognizing that even as we strive to be as evolved as possible, we are still unabatedly human. Forgiveness is offering grace because very rarely are people intentionally trying to hurt us. Hurt people hurt people. Therefore when we feel pain at the effect of someone else's doing, it is not personal. The hurt and the hurter whether in an intimate relationship or otherwise is not black and white. But let's be clear; forgiving someone does not mean we're letting them off the hook. Forgiving someone does not absolve them from consequences. In romantic relationships, this may result in the hurt person leaving. In a social setting, this may result in the perpetrator being prosecuted.

Compassionate forgiveness understands that we are punishing the behavior not the person. Leveraging the idiom 'hurt people hurt people', then 'healed people heal people.' Therein it can be seen as a personal and collective responsibility to position our thoughts and actions to align with healing versus perpetuating pain. For to withhold forgiveness is indeed to harbor the unnecessary burden of pain. Mark Twain said, "Forgiveness is the fragrance that the violet sheds on the heel that crushed it." In a conversation between the Dalai Lama and Archbishop Desmond Tutu, Tutu said, "I think we all have latent potential to feel sorry for people who are disfiguring humanity. Indeed, no one is incapable of forgiving, and no one is unforgivable." If the moral reasons are not enough to inspire and promote our capacity to forgive and express compassion, know too that there are health benefits in benevolence as well. "In a review of research on forgiveness and health, Everett L. Worthington Jr. and Michael Scherer found that unforgiveness seems to compromise the immune system in a number of ways, including disrupting the production of important hormones and the way that cells fight infections."

Practice:

We have two exercises for this section. First is a prayer borrowed from Marianne Williamson's *The Gift of Change*.

> *Dear God,*
> *I place my relationship with* _____
> *In your hands.*
> *May my presence be a blessing in his life.*
> *May my thoughts towards him be those of innocent and love,*
> *And may his thoughts towards me be of innocence and love.*
> *May all else be cast out.*
> *May our relationship be lifted*
> *To divine, right order*
> *And take the form*
> *That best serves Your purpose.*
> *May all unfold,*

In this and all things,
According to your will.
Amen

The second exercise is a Metta Meditation. Metta is a Buddhist prayer based on loving-kindness.

Deep breath in. Deep breath out…

May I be happy. May I be free from suffering and all the causes of suffering. May my life unfold with joy and ease. May _____ be happy. May _____ life be free from suffering and all the causes of suffering. May his life unfold with joy and ease.

Deep breath in. Deep breath out…

The final practice optimizes our capacity to harness the power of forgiveness. It comes from the book *Conscious Uncoupling.*

Sit and close your eyes. Imagine the person you need to forgive happy and smiling, and say aloud:

[The person's name], I forgive you for everything you've ever said or done to me in thought, word, or deed that caused me pain. You are free and I am

free! And, [person's name], I ask that you forgive me for anything that I ever said in thought, word, or action that caused you pain. You are free and I am free!

Thank you, God (Universe, Source), for this opportunity to forgive [person's name], and to forgive myself.

CHAPTER SEVENTEEN

Joy & Contentment

Story:

TYPICALLY UPON ROLLING out of bed, I make tea and either head towards my yoga mat or my bicycle. I find that this little routine grounds me and fills me with ample energy for the day. It has become ritual of sorts in my life. On this particular day, the sky was still a deep violet as the sun was just barely flirting with the horizon. The anticipation of watching the sunrise over the bay was bringing me so much joy. My feet hadn't even felt the pedals yet. I took my last sip of tea, placed my ceramic mug down, slipped on my sneakers, and ran downstairs to retrieve my bike from the garage. Still waking up, I was a bit confused when I didn't see my bike. I looked down to see the bike lock coiled like a sleeping snake. It had been severed down the midline by wire cutters. Someone had stolen my bike. My initial reaction was bluntly, *Aw, Shit!* But my subsequent reaction was quite different. I calmly thought of my alternatives. I could borrow a neighbors bike, slip on my rollerblades, go for a walk, or go back upstairs and unroll my yoga mat. All were fine alternatives. One thing was for sure; this person stole my bike, but they could not steal my joy. Another example happened while traveling in Peru. The trip to arrive in Cusco was arduous. I had a long layover in Bogota and another short layover in Lima. The travel time combined with jet lag had me fatigued. When I arrived to Cusco I was tired and hungry, but filled with so much joy! I couldn't wait to walk around the ancient city and eventually travel to Machu Picchu. At the airport, I gathered my bags and was approached by a man who was offering his taxi services. I hadn't yet calculated exchange rates, but I exchanged U.S. dollars in Lima, so I had cash. The taxi dropped me off at my hotel.

As I was checking in, I checked the exchange rates and realized the cab driver had ripped me off by charging me the equivalent of nearly 50 U.S. dollars for a three minute cab ride. The hotel attendant said it should have cost me about three bucks. I wasn't about to let a silly cab driver steal my joy. I unpacked, threw on a sweater, and began exploring the city.

As I was walking around, the situation crossed my mind. I thought, "Well, that's okay. I would have happily donated 50 dollars anyway (granted, not to that dishonest man, but happily to someone else) It's no big deal." Just then I looked down and lying in a shallow puddle was 50 U.S. dollars! I couldn't believe it! Not only had I saved my joy, the universe also supported me in saving 50 dollars. Countless situations like this are happening all the time. There are chances to stay content if not joyful, even when things don't go in precise accordance to our plan.

Truth:

Buddhist tradition is founded on the idea of joy and contentment. As the story goes, around 500 B.C., Siddhartha Gautama, a young prince realized endless suffering all around him. He noticed that the suffering was not exclusive to any type of person. Rich people, poor people, men, women, everyone it seemed had the capacity and in most cases, the proclivity to suffer. If not from disease, or natural disaster, then from anxiety, depression, and jealousy alike. He observed that the poor suffered because they wanted wealth. The wealthy suffered because they were scared of losing their riches. The young prince observed that no one was exempt from suffering. At the age of 29, Siddhartha left his village to traverse India in hopes of finding a way to avoid suffering. What he came to learn is that suffering begins in the mind. The mind is a constant breeding ground for reasons to suffer because the mind is attached to cravings. "Gautama's insight was that no matter what the mind experiences; it usually reacts with a craving, and craving always involves dissatisfaction. When the mind experiences something distasteful it craves to be rid of the irritation. When the mind experiences something pleasant, it craves the pleasure and will intensify. Therefore, the mind is always dissatisfied and restless." The only way to escape suffering, he discovered, was to transcend the mind. With this understanding and through disciplined practice, Siddhartha Gautama, the young prince, transcended the mind and was liberated from suffering. That's how he became 'The Buddha.' The practice that enabled the Buddha to overcome suffering was a simple question. He asked himself, "What am I experiencing now?", instead of what so many of us are conditioned to ask ourselves: "What do I wish to experience now?" or "How can I make this experience better?" In essence, what Buddha discovered was that by accepting the moment for what it is instead of imposing our beliefs about what it should be upon it, we can stay content. The Buddha teaches us that all emotions are fine. It is our attachment to an emotion that creates pain. If I am jealous, I can allow my jealousy to be and it will pass. But if I attach my opinion to the ephemeral experience of jealousy, now I have given the passing emotion more staying power. I have allowed something like jealousy (which doesn't have to be good or bad; it just is), to become a source of my own suffering. You see…contentment is allowing the moment to be as it is without craving for it to be different. According to Buddhism, this is how one stays in a contented state of mind. Joy, to a large degree, is a faculty of the mind.

In *The Book of Joy* the Dalai Lama said, "When something good is happening, we are happy... When these things stop, then we feel bored, restless, and unhappy. Of course this is not new. Even in the time of the Buddha, people would fall into the trap of thinking that scenery experiences would bring them happiness. I always say to people, you have to pay more attention to the mental level of joy and happiness. Not just the physical pleasure, but the satisfaction at the level of the mind. This is true joyfulness. When you are joyful and happy at the mental level, physical pain does not matter very much. But if there is no joy and happiness at the mental level, too much worrying, too much fear, then even physical comforts and pleasure will not soothe the mental discomfort."

YOU SEE...CONTENTMENT IS ALLOWING THE MOMENT TO BE AS IT IS WITHOUT CRAVING FOR IT TO BE DIFFERENT.

The Dalai Lama's sentiment here resonated so deeply with me in regards to self-love. I was boy crazy for so long. And it's because I was crazy. What's more insane than not loving yourself? Applying the Dalai Lama's passage, I was essentially placing my joy in the hyperbolic hands of another. If he loved me in the ways I was craving. I was joyful. When that love stopped, my joy vanished. At the level of mind; I did not love myself. I was constantly chasing sensory and physical feedback to compensate for the void at the level of the mind. I was in a state of constant craving. But now that I have aligned with a stable and satisfactory state of loving myself, my joy is no longer at the whims or disposal of any sensory or physical entity. Joy is within. Self-love is within.

Practice:

For this section we have to practice. The first practice here is to pose the question, "What am I experiencing now?" Just sit, breathe, ask the question, and see what comes up for you. Whatever comes up, let that be part of the experience. If the thinking mind starts to travel down a storyline, go back to the question, "What am I experiencing now?" If the mind is busy and tries to come up with assorted thoughts, acknowledge the thoughts. You can say, "Thinking. Thinking." Then return again to the question, "What am I experiencing now?" The aim of this practice is to become aware of the mind's tendency to create cravings when indeed the experience is already grounds for contentment if not for the minds attempt to intrude with false cravings. With practice, we cultivate a presence that allows us to transcend the craving. Remember, Buddha didn't become Buddha overnight. Be patient with your sweet self.

The second practice is borrowed from *The Book of Joy* written by two religious leaders, and Nobel Peace Prize Laureates, respectively the Dalai Lama from the Buddhist teachings and Archbishop Desmond Tutu from the Christian traditions. This practice is titled: *Cultivating The Eight Pillars of Joy*. This practice is based on cultivating a, "Long Distance," a "Wider Perspective," as called by the Dalai Lama. Modern science coins it as "Self-Distancing." The Archbishop calls it "God's-Eye" vantage points. Call it what you will. The aim is to use meditation to shift from our reactive emotional brain into our reflective, more evolved state of mind. There are four steps:

1. Think about a problem or situation you are facing.

2. Describe your problem as if it were happening to someone else—using your name rather than the words I, me, or mine.

3. Imagine this problem from the perspective of a week, a year, or even a decade from now. Will this issue or event still have an impact on you? Will you even remember it? What will you have learned from this experience?

4. Witness your life from a God's-eye or universal perspective. See your fears and your frustrations from this point of view. Now see all other people who are involved as having equal value and being worthy of love and respect. Then ask what will serve the whole.

CHAPTER EIGHTEEN

Manifesting & Allowing

Story:

I AM A pro manifestor. It all started with vision boards. The act of going through magazines, cutting out images that you'd like to see appear in your own life, and sticking them to a poster. I can't say with conviction that I "believed" in the concept, but I enjoyed arts and crafts. I found the activity in and of itself calming and inspiring. The end product was always a collage of things one found attractive. *Couldn't hurt,* I thought. Years after creating one specific vision board I was cleaning out my closet and stumbled upon it. A picture of a sky blue cottage with white shutters and a red door caught me eye. Just a few months prior I led a yoga retreat in Maine. We stayed in a sky blue cottage with white shutters and a red door. There's no way I could have known that would come into fruition years in advance. Then I noticed the picture of a dark brown dog with saggy cheeks. His little pink tongue hung out. He was wearing a helmet with the letters "MANG" (I think it was going to say mango, but the last letter got cut off) on it. Upon finding this vision board, I had since become the handler of a dark brown Boxer pup, known for his saggy cheeks and little pink tongue. His name was Magnum (not far off). These kinds of occurrences have been made obvious to me thousands of times since I've learned about our ability to manifest. An interesting little manifestation happened even in the course of writing this book. In one of the earlier chapters that I wrote six to nine months ago, I used Cuba as an example in the chapter about comparison and judgement. At the time, Cuba was not on my radar for my own future travels. Six to nine months later, I booked a trip on whim. Where to? Cuba. You see, consciously or not we put ideas into the universe.

On the quantum level, ideas are particles, and once placed in motion they materialize into matter. Essentially, every thought or idea is an invitation for that thought or idea to come into fruition in our lives.

IT IS NOT WHAT WE SEE THAT MATTERS. IT IS THE WAY WE'RE LOOKING THAT MATTERS MOST.

Abraham Maslow said, "The ancestor to every experience is a thought." Manifestation works most beneficially in our lives when we are intentional about what we are inviting in. As the theory goes, the universe does not receive messages in negatives. Therefore, if one thinks or declares, "I never want to date an asshole." The universe doesn't hear the "never" part. What the universe hears is "I want to date an asshole." Therefore, we should always state our intentions in the positive. Remember your thought, idea, or intention is an invitation. Similar to if you were going to throw a party and send out invitations, you would want to be accurate and specific. For example, "I am going to travel to Japan this spring." Playing with one's ability to manifest, i.e. Create one's own reality strengthens our capacity to believe in the concept. For no other reason than we see that it works.

I was reading a book on relationships that was explaining an exercise where you write down the qualities you want in a partner. That is step one. But what I found intriguing about this exercise was in step two. Step two said, next to the quality, write down the way that quality will make you feel. For example, I wrote 'Intelligent'', then next to intelligent, I wrote the way that would make me feel, 'Stimulated!' Then I wrote 'emotionally available.' How would that make me feel? 'Safe.' Below that, 'Spontaneous.' Next to that, 'Adventurous' and so on. Within days of making this list that must have had at least twenty-some items (after all, I've learned to be specific), a partner arrived in my life that exemplified all of the qualities I had noted. After investing time and energy to get to know him on a deeper level, I realized he checked off all the boxes, so to speak. There was one glitch. This man had a serious health issue. He was indeed intelligent, adventurous, emotionally available, in addition to honest, kind, attractive, affectionate, and all the other qualities I dreamt about. But I had failed to mention, 'Healthy.' Now, did I manifest an unhealthy person into my life simply because I forgot to write down the word healthy? No, likely not. I think more so, what this exercise allowed me to do was SEE the qualities that were of value to me. By being intentional about what I wanted and what I knew I deserved, I put on the proverbial goggles that highlighted my ability to notice, acknowledge, and appreciate what was available to me. As the adage goes, "seek and you will find." My list didn't "create" anything outside of myself. What my list did was amplify the signals of receptivity within me. I believe we have unlimited options available to us in any given moment. By using our powers of being intentional and manifesting, we help steer the ship towards the options of our choosing. If conversely, we are unconscious to our thought patterns we will continue to see the world through the same proverbial glasses we've always worn. Which is why some of us feel stuck or like we keep attracting the same types of people and dramas into our lives. It's because, that's indeed what we're doing.

We recall from previous chapters that the world we see is a projection of our minds. If the script in my mind says, "Being single isn't fun. Dating is hard. Everyone I meet has baggage." That will be my truth. But if I change my script to, "I enjoy spending quality time with myself. Meeting new people is fun. And plenty of kind, complete, and wonderful partners exist for me." Then that is what I'll see and experience. You see, the outer world doesn't change. It's not what we see that matters. It's the way we're looking at it that matters most. Now, as we established early on, one of my intentions for writing this book was to try to understand comprehensive concepts around what was inhibiting me from finding the right partner and establishing a sustainable, loving relationship. I wanted to learn what I was doing wrong, and discover how to do it right. It didn't take long to uncover that my true motivation wasn't to "find love." My pure motivation was to **be** in love. First and foremost to be in love with myself. As my awareness has expanded, I've come to learn that nothing outside of myself was or ever will be missing. Even more exciting yet, I've come to learn that nothing inside myself was or will ever be missing. The enigmatic little piece that I was "missing" was not something that I needed to manifest. The missing piece wasn't even something I needed to find, and surely not something that needed to be fixed. The missing piece was something I needed to ALLOW.

What has flooded my heart with immense peace and joy is this: *I have allowed myself to love myself.* I have given myself permission to be who I am, as I am, where I am, always. There is nothing missing. There is nothing to fix. There is nothing to find. There is not even anything I have to create. If I choose to do or create something it is for my own enjoyment. Nothing is a necessity. I have allowed myself the ability to simply be. And my friend, if you have not done this for yourself yet, I can not urge you. This is your journey. But my earnest wish for all of us is to give ourselves this gracious allowance. I still find joy in consciously choosing my thoughts and seeing what I can 'manifest' in my life. I still find our ability to select the goggles through which we see the world fascinating. I feel empowered in knowing that we have the capacity to shape shift the universe around us through the faculties of the mind. But what brings me peace now is allowing. Allowing to me, means making myself vibrationally available to whatever is and is to come. Since allowing brings me unsurmountable peace, part of my thinking mind is curious as to why I didn't allow it before. But the truth is, it doesn't matter. Perhaps for me, in this specific journey, in this specific incarnation, I desired to learn about allowing through its opposites. Maybe I needed to learn through mechanisms of control (fear). Maybe I needed to be at the commands of an overbearing ego. Maybe resisting was my portal to allowing. In any case, now I allow. Now, I allow myself to move through this experience of being fully human in a way that flows and organically unfolds. I know I am allowing when I am at peace. I have learned that signs of disallowance for me feels like anxiety. When I feel anxious, I know fear is present. This fear is clogging up the currents of allowance. When this happens again, there is nothing to find or fix. Even when fear is present, there is nothing missing. There is nothing wrong. I have discovered in myself that when I am not at peace. I am not allowing.

And I needn't do anything except for give myself time and space to ground and connect. I have come to understand that to be in a state of allowing I need only to be connected to the Source energy that resides within me. This source energy is what enables me to trust, love, exhibit, and embody peace. There is an intersection where manifesting and allowing share sacred ground. We can use our intentions to create a desired outcome, but then we can back up and breathe, and allow that intention to flow organically. The outcome that comes into fruition might indeed vary from the outcome we had in mind when we planted the seed of our intention; but what surfaces as a result of allowing with me the fruits of peace. We can can have faith in our intentions and then trust the process of allowing. For example, even while writing this book. I had the intention of sharing ways to love fearlessly through personal anecdotes, a collage of wisdom teachings from around the world and ages, in conjunction with practical exercises. I knew I wanted to manifest a book people could hold in their hands that would help open their hearts. What I didn't (and still don't) know is what this book will look like. Will there be cover art? What will be the scheme of the font and format? Will people want to read this book? Will it be distributed throughout the world, or will it be a scared little project that very few pay witness to? There is a line in the Vedas that says, "Do your best and release the result." This is in essence what it means to manifest and allow. Set an intention. Do your best, but then release (all control) of the result. Allow. This parlays so sweetly into relationships. For me, I still have the intention of meeting a wonderful partner. I have the intention of creating a fulfilling and sustainable relationship based on love, mutual respect, and joy. But I no longer feel the need to actively seek this person with any degree of ambition or force. (Going on fifteen dates in a matter of a few months was forceful ambition indeed.) That approach isn't wrong per say; it just no longer interests me. What interests me now is keeping an intention in my heart as I allow the process to be revealed to me within moments of peace.

Truth:

We have several ways of looking at this "truth"… with the underpinning theme that there is no absolute truth here. The intention is to widen our lens so we can witness our experiences from multiple vantage points. From there we can align our thoughts and actions to align with whatever angle we resonate with. There are no right answers here. Our three vantage points here will be belief, philosophy/religion, and science.

Belief:

When we're speak about manifesting, essentially we're talking about the law of attraction. The law of attraction has become more mainstream thanks to rather rudimentary iterations such as *The Secret,* as well as more in-depth analysis and insights through volumes such as *The Law of Attraction,* by Jerry and Esther Hicks. The Hicks are actually the transcribers and orators of knowledge that comes from an entity known as Abraham through Esther Hicks. The general belief explained through the law of attraction, or our ability to act as co-creators in our reality is based on the philosophy that positive or negative thoughts generate positive or negative experiences in our lives. From this vantage point, we can understand our lives to be blank canvases and the thoughts we generate perpetuate an energy that draws the same energy magnetically closer until it lands upon our canvas. In this way we use our thoughts to color our lives. This is not to say that if I dream of a red BMW that a red BMW will magically appear in my life. The law of attraction is not intended, nor does it function as a genie lamp that grants us magic wishes. The law of attraction rather illustrates a mental paradigm where we can prime our thoughts to call forth and exhibit particular qualities in our lives, so long as our peripheral thoughts, words, and deeds are also in alignment. While some might assume this to be a pseudoscience that is not based on fact or evidence, one could say that same about the stock market. The stock market, law enforcement, government agencies, and a myriad of other trusted systems function effectively not because they were proven empirically, but because enough people chose to believe in them and place their trust in them. The stock market will crash if enough people abandon their faith in it. Complete anarchy could break out if people decide laws aren't worth believing in. The government can (and has) just shut down because citizens choose not to cooperate with the agreed upon system. You see, many concepts that we blindly assume are tried and true are actually just concepts. Not all things that are valuable are absolute laws. Some laws such as gravity do not require our faith to be uninterruptedly effective. But other systems that are just as valuable such as family values, equal rights, and religion do require some level of belief. In my opinion, anything that supports our quality of life, enhances the evolution of consciousness, and promotes goodness in the world, rather it be through science or faith, is equally honorable. Essentially, the hallmark aim in manifestation is the aim to create a fulfilling and noble life. Ralph Waldo Emerson said, "The only person you are destined to become is the person you decide to be." In many ways declaring our intention, using affirmations plant the seed of our intentions, and then visualizing that intention as though it has come into reality is essentially a cognitive framing device that is built not on hopeful thinking or spiritual magnetism, but more so on cultivating confidence and conviction to become who we have decidedly chosen to become. Sages through the ages have mimicked this concept. Buddha said, "What you think you become. What you feel you attract. What you imagine, you create." Spiritual teacher Bashar said, "You can have anything you want, when you give up the belief you can't have it." Manifestation is not an "ask and you shall receive" zero sum game. Manifestation or the law of attraction is a tool that allows us to train our minds to become machines that generate high frequency thoughts that have the capability to call forth, recognize, and appreciate high frequency experiences.

Philosophy/Religion:

Danish Philosopher Kierkegaard said, "If you name me, you negate me, by giving me a name, a label, you negate all the other things I could be. You lock the particle into being a thing by pinning it down, naming it, but at the same time you are creating it, defining it to exist." Creativity is our highest nature. with creating things comes time, which creates the illusion of solidity. Advance meditators know stillness is the greatest power. Buddha had a name for this phenomena—Kalapas, or tiny particles, or wavelets that are arriving and passing away trillions of times per second. Reality is a series of frames in a holographic film camera moving quickly as to create the illusion of continuity. When consciousness becomes perfectly still. The illusion is understood because it is consciousness itself that drives the illusion.

In ancient traditions of the East, it has been understood for thousands of years that all is vibration. Nada Bahama means the universe is sound. Nada—sound or vibration, Brahma—the name for God. Brahma simultaneously is the universe, Is the creator. The artist and the art are inseparable. The Upanishads, an ancient text from India, depicts Brahma sitting on a lotus. Brahma opens his eyes and the world comes into being. He closes his eyes and the world goes out of being. You never see anything in its totality because it is made up of layer of vibration and it is constantly changing because it is drinking in Akasha (space—unlimited potential). Native Americans believed, "Everything has spirit," which is to say everything is connected to the one vibratory source. There is one consciousness. One field. One vibratory force that moves through all. This field is not happening around you. This force is happening through you and as you. You are the you in universe. You are the eyes through which creation sees itself. When you wake from a dream you realize everything in the dream was you. You were creating it. So called real life is no different. Everyone everything is you. The one consciousness looking out of every eye.

Science:

Researchers at The European Organization for Nuclear Research, CERN, in Geneva Switzerland announced that they found the Higgs Boson, or God particle. The experiment proved scientifically that an invisible energy field fills the vacuum of space. Standard models cannot account for how particles get their mass. Everything appears to be made of vibration. But there is no thing being vibrated. It is as if there has been a hidden dancer; a shadow dancing in the ballet of the universe, and all the other dancers have always danced around the hidden dancer. We have observed the choreography of that dance, but until now we could not see that dancer. Science is approaching the threshold between consciousness and matter. The eye with which we look at the primordial field and the eye through which the field looks at us are one and the same.

Albert Einstein said, "Everything is energy and that's all there is to it. Match the frequency of your reality you want and you can not help but get that reality. It can be no other way. It is not philosophy. It is physics." Now, what I've found in my experience is that it is possible to generate high frequency thoughts, set intentions, state affirmations, and visualize until the cows come home, and yet... Waiting. Waiting. Waiting...This is where the practice of allowing becomes paramount. When we are in alignment and things are not going as "planned", as in accordance with our agenda, that does not mean that we are not going to plan. There is always a wider perspective, that our thinking mind, frankly, can not see. To me, attempting to manifest something and coming up short and declaring it a loss is like being on the edge of your seat wholeheartedly invested in a really good movie, then when the actor says something you didn't expect or don't agree you, you jump up and storm out of the theater. We haven't seen the whole movie yet. The stories of our lives are still in motion. Yes, we are the leading stars, senior producers and directors, but there is an even grander visionary behind this cinema and sometimes we have to be at peace with that. The peace comes through allowing. The position of allowing is actually easeful. The act of surrender is calming and pleasant. The "grander visionary" here is synonymous with as described by the researchers who discovered the Higgs Boson or God particle, "the hidden dancer; a shadow, dancing in the ballet of the universe." It is the enigmatic quality that drives the universe that is currently ineffable. And the peace that I describe as coming from the state of allowance is as far as I can see, similar to "the power of stillness," that great meditators and the Buddha speak of. This process of quieting the conscious mind that is incessantly creating projections that are infallibly changing.

Practice:

We'll have two practices for this section: one for manifesting and one for allowing. We'll play with the art of manifesting through creating a vision board. First, collect a stack of magazine. Choose magazines that are filled with images that pertain to your interests. For example, if you're interested in taking a trip around the world, collect travel magazines. If your desire is to open a restaurant, include a few culinary magazines in your stack. If you want to get married, perhaps pick up a bridal magazine. Once you have your stack of magazines, go through them one by one and select images that appeal to you. Cut them out. Create a new stack of images that inspire and delight you. You can choose to cut out words and phrases as well. The next step is adhering the images onto a poster board. You can use any size poster board. Compose the images in a way that is visual exciting and that can elicit a feeling of joy within you when you look at your board. Use glue or a glue stick for this process. Finally, hang or place your vision board in a place where you will readily see it, such as on your closet door, next to your refrigerator or coffee machine, or in your office near your computer. All of the images you chose are charged with a vibration.

The concept in creating a vision board is that when you are exposed to the vibration of your choosing on a regular basis, your molecular chemistry synchronizes with that frequency. Another reason is by placing these visual representations of potential realities in your field, you have essentially planted the seed for these potentials to come into fruition. Have fun with it! The next exercise is on the process of Allowing, or as the Dalai Lama and Archbishop Desmond Tutu call it, Acceptance. This practice has been borrowed from *The Book of Joy*. As the designers of this meditation come from a Buddhist and Christian backgrounds respectively, this includes elements of both religions.

Acceptance—A meditation: Any possibility of joy requires an acceptance of reality. It is the only place from which one can start to work for change, personal or global. Meditation is practice that allows us to accept our life moment to moment without judgement or the expectation of life to be other than what it is.

1. **Sit comfortably,** either in a chair with your feet on the ground, or crossed-legged. You can rest your hands on your lap.

2. **Close your eyes** and take several long breaths through your nose. Feel your stomach rise and fall as you breathe into your belly.

3. **Pay attention** to what you hear around you. Notice how the world is alive with sound. As thoughts about these noises arise—judgements, assessments, irritations—let the evaluations drift away.

4. **Release your focus** of the breath and, while staying in the present moment, notice any thoughts or feelings that arise. Perhaps you will notice some discomfort in your body or have feeling arise, or you may have a thought about what you need to accomplish or remember today.

5. **Observe the moment** without judgement. As the thoughts come up, let them float away without judging them, or getting caught up in them.

6. **Think of a situation** you are having a hard time accepting (allowing to happen). Perhaps it is difficulty finding a job or life partner, or it may be a friend's illness or a collective reality such a war.

7. **Remind yourself** that it is the nature of reality. These painful realities do happen to us, to those we love, and in our world.

8. **Acknowledge** the fact that you cannot know all the factors that have led to this event.

9. **Accent what has happened** has already happened. There is nothing you can do to change the past.

10. **Remind yourself:** "In order to make a positive contribution in this situation, I must accept the reality of its existence."

You can also choose to reflect on or recite one of the following passages, one from the Buddhist tradition, the other from the Christian tradition:

> *If something can be done about it,*
> *what is the need for dejection?*
> *And if nothing can be done about it,*
> *what use is there for being dejected?*
>
> —*Shantidevi, The Way of the Bodhisattva*

God, give us the grace to accept with serenity

the things that cannot be changed,

courage to change the things

which should be changed,

and the wisdom to distinguish

the one from the other.

—*Reinhold Niebuhr, The Serenity Prayer*

CHAPTER NINETEEN

Ground & Connect (to Intuition)

Story:

MY HOME STATE of Florida is said to be the lightning capital of the world. As a kid, I enjoyed watching lightning storms. The unorganized dance of wild energy zapping through the sky. Light racing across the horizon and bolting down from above. Sitting safe in the comfort of shelter, I was mesmerized by the movement in the sky; the way it seemed as random as it was powerful. Sometimes I feel like that lightning...frantic, ungrounded, and potentially destructive. I know this electric feeling well. For me, it feels like a quick pulsation in my chest, a hurried heartbeat, thoughts that travel at a zillion miles an hour, ideas that come too fast to logically firm up. It's an excitable, intense, and oftentimes uncomfortable energy. This energy has been with me as long as I can remember. It would be altogether easy to be frightened by this jolted undercurrent. If I didn't know better, I'd call it anxiety. But if this journey has taught me anything, it's that the energy that is often misunderstood as fear is actually the energy of light. Our light is as brilliantly captivating as the electricity that fills up a Florida thunderstorm sky. We are energy.

THE ENERGY THAT IS OFTEN
MISUNDERSTOOD AS FEAR IS
ACTUALLY THE ENERGY OF LIGHT.

Our nervous systems are surging with electricity all the time. I've come to know that when I feel anxious, what I actually am is a buzzing body of light that craves so desperately to get grounded. For my spirit must know that the only way for my light to be useful is if I am plugged in. Imagine this: You're decorating a new space. You recognize the space to be dark so you go to the store to buy a lamp. The lamp has all the energy it needs within it to light up a room. You're driving home with the lamp in the back seat. You're envisioning where you'll place it in the room. In your mind, you can imagine how it'll illuminate and complete the feel and function of your new space. You get home and place the lamp in the corner. The room stays dark. Why? Because you forgot to plug it in. We're no different from the lamp. We have everything we need within us to illuminate our lives and the world around us. But here's the catch, we don't function properly if we're not plugged in.

Being plugged in means getting grounded. Excess stimulation, technology, and activity in our schedules dial the voltage of our nervous systems up so high we quiver in our own skin. Being grounded means reconnecting to the earth and to the quiet space within us that knows truth. The voice of truth is the voice of our higher Self or our intuition. The voice of intuition is wise. She speaks succinctly. Our intuition offers us clarity and guidance. It is always with us, but we can not hear her if we are not grounded. When we're grounded, we're connected to Self, and the truth of who we are. The truth of who we are is that we are worthy, lovable, and fearless beings. I drove home from work one evening. I had a typical day consumed by a commute, conversations with clients, emails, several cups of caffeine, admittedly, a few quick glances at social media, and it was now being punctuated by the occasional honks and echoes of passing sirens as I sat in bumper-to-bumper traffic. My car was pretty much at a standstill, but my nervous system was running a marathon. My mind was lapping the stillness of my body. I felt anxious. I knew I needed to get grounded. I decided to get off the busy road and take the back way home. I knew it would take longer, but it would be quiet. I took a deep breath, turned right to escape the trail of brake lights, and took the alternative route down a cobble stoned road. Rather than passing the neighborhood park in a rush to get home, I pulled over. My only agenda was to get grounded. I didn't know what that would look like or what would come of it, but my nervous system was telling me it was necessary. I parked, got out of my car, found a patch of grass that seemed to be clear of spiky weeds or bugs, and I sat down facing a little pond. I instantly felt the rough texture of the grass through my cotton dress. I noticed the temperature in the air, the absence of sound, the song of a passing bird. I appreciated the warmth of the late afternoon sun on my skin. I noticed the glassy water and the trails of ripples from the ducks that moved passed. I closed my eyes. I took three deep breaths. I kept my eyes close until my heartbeat became slow and rhythmic. The mania in my mind slowed down. Within minutes I had shifted from an erratic lightning storm to a plugged in lamp. Just sitting there on the ground at the end of a long day had saved me from feeling like I was buzzing in my skin, to feeling at home in my skin.

A few minutes later, feeling settled, I returned to my car. As I continued my journey home, I heard my intuition. I don't know why per say, (maybe so I could share it with you now), but something in me told me to grab my phone. I grabbed my phone, hit record, and started to talk. This is what my Self said…

Here's what you have learned about love. Well little one, you have learned a lot since you started. Mostly you learned how to forget everything the world taught you; because you were all knowing the moment you entered. You came here to teach love. You forgot along the way, but the the pain that came from forgetting was part of the plan to motivate you to remember. You've learned that you don't need to earn anyone's love. That you don't need to prove that you are worthy, or that you are deserving to anyone, specifically yourself. You've learned that you'll never have to change to become lovable. That there's nothing you have to do, or say. You don't need to become. You are already. You have learned that love is not retractable. You have learned that love doesn't come from the heart. Not from that one isolated space that you think of anyway. Love is in every cell of your being. It is in the molecule and the in little specs that form each molecule inside each cell. You have learned that you can not do anything other than love because that is what you are. Even when you're angry. Even when you say things that seem like the absolute antithesis of love; that too is love. You have learned to see through other people. You have learned to see through fears. Fears have become invisible to you; more clear than glass. Glass you can run into. You can't walk through glass, but fear, you walk through those. You have learned that love comes in quiet times. You've learned that the louder, the more lusty, and the more dramatic it feels, that's the scared kind of love. It has taken you a moment, but you have uncovered true love. You have finally found it within yourself. When you look in the mirror, you no longer see your body. You don't even see your skin so much. You can see your soul again. You've missed her. You have learned to love adults the way you love babies. That innocence; that inarticulate, that messy, that adorable love. You have learned to love adults the way you love babies…even the ones who don't know how to express themselves. You see the adults who throw temper tantrums as innocent children. You see them as the love they are. The love they are scared to recognize. This you have learned of love. You have learned that you can find love in everyone. That everyone is a reflective surface…recently Windexed, spotlessly shiny. You recognize their flaws as holograms, as other dimensions and angles to see your own love. Your love is most tested my dear, when you are tired. So when you are tired, close your eyes. Let sleep restore your heart. You have come here to do exactly what you came here to do…to be love. And you're no longer scared because you know that no one can ever take that away from you. You know that you can give and give, endlessly, relentlessly, and people can take it; but nothing can ever be taken from you. Your wholeness is holy. Unshakable. You have done well. You have finally learned to love yourself.

That's all she said. I hit stop on the voice recorder on my phone. I arrived at home, took a bath, ate dinner, crawled in bed, and slept. That day might have ended so differently; this book might have ended so differently had I not taken the time to get grounded. It's taken me years of being ungrounded to fully appreciate the peace that comes with being grounded. I have come to adopt the practice of grounding as a direct passage towards connecting with Self and my intuition. We have learned that the thinking mind and ego can not always be trusted; but the intuition—yes, she is always knowing. When I'm connected to my intuition the outside world becomes smaller and less significant. The erroneous voice of the ego becomes muted in contrast to the quiet voice of the intuition who gets her point across, not in volume, but in relevance.

Here is what I know when I listen to my intuition. I know that nothing outside of myself, no external element is going to abolish my fear and free my heart. Fearlessness is an inside job.

I KNOW THAT NO EXTERNAL ELEMENT IS GOING TO ABOLISH MY FEAR AND FREE MY HEART. FEARLESSNESS IS AN INSIDE JOB.

Everything I need to live as freely as possible is within me. The only person who can soothe my soul and unlock the abyss of unconditional love that was gifted to me with the intention of being enjoyed and shared with others, is me. I am accountable for my contribution and response to every relationship in which I engage. And the most vital relationship for me to engage in is the one with my Self. When my relationship with Self is solid, every other relationship I invest in becomes more valuable.

I think the pervasive and underlining fear that plagues us all is the fear of not being worthy. This fear may indeed just be part of the human experience. Assuming I have any authority over telling myself or anyone else how to completely eradicate the surfacing of this little gremlin thought may be egregiously ambitious. I started and I'm closing this book with appreciating that I do not have all the answers. None of us do. Not having all the answers, yet seeking and asking questions with the aim to grow could very well be one of the reasons we're all here. Paradoxically, our fears might be a driving impetuous in fulfilling that purpose. Our fears might be needles on the compass of growth. Equipped with mindfulness and confidence in our ability to use fears, not let them use us. Kept in right amounts, fears may indeed have a small rightful place in our lives. But what I know for sure, is that I have autonomy over my thoughts. And any fear-based thought that snowballs into self-limiting behaviors that detracts from joy and ability to love myself and others needs to be dismantled and disempowered. I have the power and tools to shape my perspective so that I can see the world and move through the world with eyes of love. I don't get to choose the lessons I'm here to learn, but I can curate my thoughts and perspective in a way that allows me to learn through joy versus suffering. I—we all—have the faculty to mitigate unnecessary pain by inverting the fears that work to confiscate our joy. The ego, comparison, judgement, and perfectionism weaken as we become grounded in the Self, and fortify our connection to our own intuition. The truth is I will inevitably fumble. Being perfect at being fearless is an oxymoron because perfection in of itself is one of the guises of fear. What I will be is imperfectly fearless. I'll move as my Self guides me. I'll listen to my intuition. I'll remain vibrationally available to the experiences presented to me. I'll do my best to align my thoughts and actions to be in congruence with my understanding of fearlessness. For me, fearlessness is being unencumbered and un-crippled by thoughts that bind me to smallness. Knowing I have…we all have, unrestricted access to this state, I think it is incumbent upon us to love fearlessly.

Truth:

Ancient Eastern traditions teach us carried by the practices of yoga and Ayurveda teach us that we all have a "third eye," or intuition housed in the Ajna Chakra. Chakras are wheels or reservoirs of energy that govern various physiological and psychological responses in the body. Just as the liver is responsible for detoxifying chemicals and metabolizing drugs, and the kidneys facilitate the filtering of blood and the removal of waste, our Chakras exist to carry out very particular jobs.

WHAT I WILL BE IS
IMPERFECTLY FEARLESS.

The Ajna Chakra is located at the back of the brain, the place where the optic nerves cross. That's why it's called the third eye. It corresponds with our pineal gland. This reservoir of energy is connected to the subconscious mind and is the seat of our intuition. When we quiet the mind through the process of removing excess stimulation while shifting our focus from the outside world to the inside world, we access our ability to connect with our higher Self. The practice of grounding and turning inward is what connects us to our intuition. Practically speaking, if we're running around like busy bees performing various tasks all day, our brains are consumed with analytics and processes to actively receive and process the wisdom that dwells within. Wisdom is always within us. It communicates

through our intuition; and while our intuition is clear, she is not demanding. If we don't deliberately check in with her, we can all too easily miss what she has to offer. Not recognizing the power of the intuition, or bypassing her because, "we don't have time," is a criminal in respect to becoming fearless. For our intuition offers us every truth we need to dispel and rise above our fears.

Practice:

1. This practice is called Ajna Nidra. It is a guided meditation that mimics the rejuvenate benefits of sleep while promoting access to our third eye. I would recommend reading this aloud slowly while recording it on your phone or device; that way when you want to connect you can simply lie down in a comfortable place where you won't

be interrupted; from there press play and enjoy the pleasant experiencing of grounding and connecting to your intuition.

Lie down comfortably. Place a pillow under your head and knees. Use as many blankets and props as you need to make your body completely comfortable. Be sure your warm, as you body temperature will drop as you relax. The sixth Chakra is also known as the third eye Chakra. Imagine a wheel of energy between the eyebrows. Anna Chakra rules the eyes, ears, nose, sense of self, and the nervous system. The world Ajna translates as center of command; keeping all the other Chakras in tune. The mantra or sound for this Chakra is OM. Here the sound resonating as I chant it now, OM. OM. OM. When Ajna is closed poor memory, loss of focus, and lack of insight may result. Life seems black and white and the big picture may be lost. Too much energy in the third eye may result in intellectual arrogance and dogmatic in their thinking. Balanced Ajna energy helps to maintain balance throughout all systems. Inner vision, self-awareness, and psychic awareness are all gifts from the third eye. The practice of Yoga Nidra to balance Ajna Chakra begins now. Maybe sure you're completely comfortable. Feel your head and neck relax into its support. Soften the face, eyes, and forehead. Close the eyes and feel the whole body find stillness and relaxation.

Sense breath and energy being softly directed to the space between the eyebrows. Feel the chaos of daily life fade into the background. Bring your awareness to your nostrils. Focus on your left breath. Feel the air flow in and out of your left nostril. Feel the breath flow in the left nostril to the third eye point. Imagine the breath filled with cooling silver-blue moon light. Keep your awareness on the silver-blue light flowing as the breath through the left nostril. (give one minute pause). Now, bring your awareness to the right nostril. Feel the sensation of the breath flowing in and out of the right nostril. Imagine this breath filled with warm-golden sunlight. Follow the path on the inhale through the right nostril up to the third eye and out. (give one minute pause.) Now, breathe through both nostrils for a few cycles of breath. Now inhale through the left and exhale through the right. Inhale through the right and exhale left. Continue inhale left, exhale right. Inhale right, exhale left. This alternate nostril breathing helps to balance the polarities of the two hemispheres of the brain. Continue watching the breath inhale left, exhale right for a few more cycles. While you do this, set your intention. Your intention aligns your deepest desires with your actions in the world. Also say to yourself, I am practicing yoga nidra. I will not sleep. I am relaxed. Now, we scan the body with progressive relaxation. Begin with the left side of the body in the left nostril. Left eye, eyebrow, left hemisphere of the brain. Ear. Left side of the throat, collar bone, left chest. Armpit, front of the upper arm, inner elbow, inner forearm, inside of the wrist, palm of the hand, left hand thumb, first finger, second finger, third finger, fourth finger, back of the left hand, back of the wrist, utter forearm, elbow point, back of the upper arm, shoulder blade, left rib cage, waist, hip, buddock, back of the thigh, back of the knee, calf, ankle, heel, sole of the foot, left big toe, second toe, third toe, fourth toe, fifth toe. Top of the left foot, front of the ankle, shin, kneecap, front of the thigh, left groin, the pelvic floor, the entire left side of the body. Entire left side of the body. Entire left side of the body. Move to the right side of the body beginning with the right nostril. Right eye, eyebrow, right hemisphere of the brain. Ear. Right side of the throat, collar bone, right chest. Armpit, front of the upper arm, inner elbow, inner forearm, inside of the wrist, palm of the hand, right hand thumb, first finger, second finger, third finger, fourth finger, back of the right hand, back of the wrist, utter forearm, elbow point, back of the upper arm, shoulder blade, right rib cage, waist, hip, buttock, back of the thigh, back of the knee, calf, ankle, heel, sole of the foot, right big toe, second toe, third toe, fourth toe, fifth toe. Top of the right foot, front of the ankle, shin, kneecap, front of the thigh, right groin, the pelvic floor, the entire right side of the body. Entire right side of the body. Entire right side of the body. Move to the space between the eyebrows, the nose, upper lip, lower lip, chin, jaw, throat, sternum, upper abdomen, navel, lower belly, floor of the pelvis, tail bone, sacrum, the entire spine, back of the neck, back of the head, crown of the head, forehead, the space between the eyebrows, the center of the body, the entire body. Your whole body. Make sure that you are awake and can hear the sound of the guiding voice. Imagine complete darkness; the blackness of space...a night without moon or stars. What feelings reside in this space of darkness where nothing can be seen?

From the darkness emerge into the light. A bright candle flame, the warmth of sunlight, a flashlight leading the way...notice if different emotions reside here where everything is revealed. Can darkness and light exist simultaneously? Imagine living in a world where you can not see. Truth is kept from you. There is a veil blocking everything, and you can not see. Now imagine the opposite. There is light. You see opportunity. The veil has been lifted. Your perspective is expansive and you can see. Now imagine both together. Dualities that exists at the same time. Imagine non-duality, nothing is either all good or all bad. There are always shades of nuances. You perceive the oneness of all things beyond any doubt. Can these two concepts exist at the same moment? Stare at the dark space in front of your closed eyes. Imagine that you are sitting in front of a movie screen. You are alone. This is your personal sitting room. Upon the screen you see images begin to take shape. Notice what is there without judgement, and without guiding the flow of images. The images are a gift from your consciousness. Stay detached as the images reveal themselves. Imagine the symbol OM, a flash of bright light, an indigo sky, a deep still lake, the space between the eyebrows, a

*marriage ceremony, a question mark, the dictionary,
a thick forest…a pair of eyeglasses, the darkness
of space, A tall mountain, a shooting star, a movie
theater, the smooth stones at the bottom of a clear
mountain stream, ancient texts, this room, a clock
face, a sailing ship…a fortune teller with a crystal
ball, a double helix, a wizard's cap…a telescope,
holding the hand of a loved one, a glittering gem
under murky water…your body lying on the floor…
return your awareness to your eye brown center, and
imagine sitting on the edge of a deep still lake. Spend
time creating the space around the lake. Is the shore
rocky or smooth? You are on a boat in the lake.
You are observing the environment. The deep blue
sky, the shoreline you created, the movement of the
water…these nuances represent the landscape of the
mind. Are the waves small or big. Hear the waves;
is it quiet or is the water crashing. Breathe deep
breaths in and full breaths out. Watch the surface
of the water become smooth, glassy, and transparent
as you breathe. When the water is glassy, look down
and see your reflection in the water. See your calm
eyes, the gentle smile of your lips, see the reflection of
the expansive sky in the reflection of the water. See
the universe around you and within you.*

Continue to look deeper and deeper into the water trying to see the very bottom. You look very hard to see what lies in the bottom of the lake bed, but the harder you try the more movement you create on the surface of the water. As thoughts come, do not try to push them away. Just breathe to still the waters of the mind and breathe to still the movement of the water so you can see deep beneath the surface. As you watch your breathe stillness and calmness gloss over the mind and the surface of the water. Hold on to this gentle imagine as a profound inner silence comes from this space. Connect to your inner wisdom. In reality there is only now and the wisdom that is here. In this peaceful state you drift closely to shore and disembark onto the bank. It is time to repeat your intention. State it three times to yourself with your full awareness...knowing that the intention plants a seed for realizing the truth of your inner wisdom. Bring the awareness back to the sensation of your breath flowing in and out through your nostrils. Your body is resting on the floor. Feel the meeting places of your body and the surface beneath you. Notice your face, especially your lips and eyes. Gentle begin to reawaken by wiggling your fingers and toes. Gently hug your knees into your chest. Give yourself a gentle hug. Roll to the right and use your arms to guide yourself to a seated position. Stay relaxed as you sit up. The practice of Yoga Nidra is now complete.

2. If your time is limited, or that practice does not resonate with you, I recommend going outside, slipping off your shoes, and standing on the earth. As your bare feet meet the ground, feel the texture of the surface beneath you. Is the density of the ground soft or firm? Feel the temperature of the earth…is it warm or cool? Allow yourself to become sensitive to the sensations on the soles of your feet. Can you feel the blades of grass on your arches, the mud between your toes, or the tiny grains of sand on the edges of your heels? As you stand on the earth feel your breath in the soles of your feet. As you inhale allow the breath to rise up your shins, knees, thighs, torso, throat, face…all the way up to the crown of your head. As you exhale, allow the breath to slowly rinse down the body from head to toe. Inhale, invite the energy of the earth up the length of the body. Exhale, feel the pleasant energy gently fall down

the length of the body. Continue that breathing cycle for one minute. Inhale breath rising; exhale breath falling. A review in the Journal of Environmental and Public Health found that drawing electrons from the earth improves our health in similar respects to the ways people with chronic pain using grounding carbon fiber mattresses slept better and experienced less pain. The Journal of Alternative and Complementary Medicine found that standing on the earth barefoot increases the surface charge of red blood cells which decreases blood viscosity (one of the main factors in heart disease.) While we aim to ground for spiritual benefits, it is no surprise that the physical body benefits as well. This practice can be done multiple times a day for as long as you wish.

Adore Your Body

WE'RE TAKING A slight detour from the story, truth, tell format to talk soulfully about the body. Don't worry, I'm not going to give you, *Five Steps to Fighting Fat, Seven Steps to Sexy Abs, Ten Ways to Feel Like a Ten,* or any of that other rubbish. The goal here is to promote your ability to see your body not as a mass of muscles, fat, bones, skin, and features; but rather, to see you body as a divine vessel that so elegantly carries your magnificent soul. Ancient practices and Eastern Traditions have long known that the body and mind are not separate entities, but rather two intimately and interconnected bodies that cannot effectively be bifurcated. What happens in the body affects the mind, and what happens in the mind translate to the body. Renowned mind-body physician Deepak Chopra says, "The body is a printout of our experiences," and philosophers throughout the world reveal to us that experiences are a print out of our thoughts; therefore the body is a print out of our thoughts.

THE GOAL HERE IS TO PROMOTE YOUR ABILITY TO SEE YOUR BODY NOT AS A MASS OF MUSCLES, FAT, BONES, SKIN, AND FEATURES; BUT RATHER, TO SEE YOUR BODY AS A DIVINE VESSEL THAT ELEGANTLY CARRIES YOUR BEAUTIFUL SOUL.

The ancient teachings of yoga taught us that there are five sheaths or layers to our being, called, Koshas. According to yoga, all disease originates in the mind, travels through the energy body, and comes into fruition, or lodges itself in the physical body. Modern medicine validates this theory under through the terminology, psychosomatic; which means begins in the mind and appears in the body. Our body is constantly responding to what we're thinking. If we're anxious, the body releases adrenaline and cortisol, not as a punishment, but because its function is to support our needs. And at the primal level, if we're anxious the body assumes it is a valid threat. It provides us with a huge rush of fight or flight chemicals so that we can flee from whatever it is that's scaring us. AKA, run from the lion. But here's the catch; there is no lion. The anxiety was more often than not an effect of a deadline, overwhelming schedule, or self-limiting. *He's not calling. He doesn't like me. Crap, that client didn't respond. I guess I bombed my proposal. Cupcakes in the break-room again. No! This place is going to ruin my diet.* In all of these cases, there is no actual threat. There is only the thought or perception of threat. This makes no difference to the body. The chemical response is the same. Using this example, the adrenaline and cortisol released in reaction to the fear based thought—body flooded with adrenaline and cortisol will often hold on to extra weight to quote, cushion itself from stress. Now, what happens so often in our solution based approach is that we become so fixated on finding a way to resolve the problem that we become distracted by the problem itself.

OUR BODY IS CONSTANTLY
REINFORCING OUR THOUGHTS, AND
GIVING US TANGIBLE FEEDBACK
AS TO WHAT WE'RE THINKING.

The problem was never the body. The body is an intelligent and sympathetic container. The problem, if we want to call it that, was the fear-based thought that served as a catalyst for nothing more than a natural chain of reactions that were designed to nourish, not spoil the body. I know for me, when I used to think about myself, I first thought about my body. I identified my self worth with the container I was dwelling within. My body gave shape to my identity, rather than my soul. I find this to be true for many of us. So, for many of us, when we're unhappy with our bodies we hone into how to correct the body. This is a common, but unconscious and ineffective approach. Our body is constantly reinforcing our thoughts, giving form to our thoughts, and providing us with tangible feedback to how we're thinking. I believe we're all a little uncomfortable in our bodies from time to time. That's because we're light and ethereal spirits that reside in a dense home...the home of the human body. When we feel displeased with some particular aspect of our physical beings, it would behoove us to look inward for the solution. The body is not the problem. The body is the symptom or obvious representation of what needs attention. What needs attention will invariably be some aspect of a deep inner need. Fortunately for us, we're already uncovered ways to address our deep inner needs. We can implement the practices we've come to understand and consciously reshape our ways of thinking. As we balance and elevate our way of thinking, our body will instinctively react by returning to its balanced and elevated state.

Unhealthy eating habits, insufficient sleep, chronic inflammation, obsession with food; either through indulgence or restriction, and most of the common issues that plague our physical bodies will automatically soften as we learn to love ourselves. A person who loves themselves naturally makes healthful choices. A person who love themselves recognizes that they are not the body, but that they are a valuable soul who is worthy of consuming healthful foods and engaging in healthful actions. Learning to love ourselves includes learning to love our bodies. Just as we've come to understand that the voices of fear in our heads are not actually gremlins, but more so parts of ourselves that need attention and to be loved. We can also comprehend that the parts of our physical bodies that can feel haunting at times, are too, not malevolent; but rather they are parts of our being that also require attention and love. The body is for all intents and purposes, outside. Attention and love will always be an inside job.

So when it comes to loving the body, I offer you this: Give yourself space and time to get in your body. It's so easy to live in our heads; constantly thinking and planning, rather than allowing us to think through our nervous system. Our nervous system provides us with an intelligent network of communication that speaks to us through pulsations, rhythms, and temperature. Integrating a daily practice of going for a walk, swim, yoga class, or sitting in nature and taking deep breaths allows us to get out of our heads and into our bodies. Once we're in our bodies we can feel and experience the messages and wisdom the body offers us.

IF WE'RE THINKING POSITIVELY ABOUT OUR BODIES, OUR BODIES BECOME UPLIFTED VESSELS THROUGH WHICH WE CAN EFFECTIVELY MOVE THROUGH THE WORLD.

Eating wholesome food advances our ability to receive vital messages from the body. Chemicals and additives found in processed foods harm our microbiomes and inhibit the cellular intelligence that carry wisdom throughout our being. Obviously, we live in modern times where fast food is ubiquitous. No one needs added pressure to completely reform their diet. It's just worth being conscious and generous towards yourself in choosing foods that support the wholeness of who you are. And finally, when it comes to loving the body—be aware of how you speak to and about your body. Your body is listening to you. On a visceral level, your body is attuned to your thoughts and feelings. If we want to love our bodies, we need to express love to our bodies. If we look in the mirror and feel the need to express opinions about what we see, let's afford ourselves the decency to formulate positive opinions. These positive thoughts will be amplified by the contagious effect of generating more positive thoughts. And we recall, the body is a print out of our thoughts. If we're thinking positively about our bodies, our bodies become uplifted vessels through which we can effectively move through the world. Independent of anything or anyone outside of ourselves; we deserve to adore and enjoy the our bodies. We deserve to feel at home in the comfort of our own skin. But it's worth noting, that as we have come to understand—everything is connected; so cultivating a healthy relationship with the physical body does indeed benefit our other relationships as well. Our physical bodies do not exist to be the place holders and punching bags in which we project our deepest fears. Our physical bodies are intelligent and divine abodes for our souls. Your body loves you. She has always loved you, and she will love you until the end of time. Go on, adore her.

In Closing…

WHEN WE'RE NEARLY INTOXICATED BY THE HARMFUL FUMES OF PERFECTION, AND WE REALIZE OUR IMPERFECTIONS ARE INDEED MAGNIFICENT, LOVE WINS.

The truth is fear is part of the human experience, but fortunately for us, so is love. Love is far and wide the strongest and most powerful force of energy on the planet. We hear stories of mothers who embody momentary superhuman strength to save their children. In times of peril, otherwise everyday pedestrians take brave leaps directly into harm's way to rescue complete strangers. We know love conquers fear. But love triumphs over fear not only during times of madness and unique scenarios, love is always stronger than fear. In quiet moments when the voice of fallacy tries to convince us we're not enough and we replace that voice with honest affirmations that reinforce our worth; love wins. When we're on the precipice of exposing all our vulnerabilities and we almost build walls to stay "safe", but we trust ourselves enough to reveal the fullness of who we are; love wins. During periods where our confidence wavers because someone else doesn't recognize our value, but we understand that someone else's opinion of us does not define who we are; love wins. When someone is hurtful and inflicts pain and we offer them compassion and forgiveness because we recognize that they only resorted to such behavior because they are hurting; love wins.

When we're nearly intoxicated by the harmful fumes of perfection, and we realize that our imperfections are indeed magnificent; love wins. In flashes of time where we're tempted to compare ourselves to others, but we recall that beyond the ego we're all the same; love wins. When we stop trying to fill perceived voids within ourselves with the company or validation of others, and in contrast recognize that everything we need to live a life of ebullience resides within; love wins.

I've spent my life fantasizing about love. I've spent years pondering fear. The process of writing this book has been at times daunting. As you would imagine, reflecting deeply on past relationships and the heavy arsenal of fear that has held me back isn't exactly a walk in the park. But this process has also been uplifting and empowering. My personal experience in writing this book has made me question my beliefs and has heightened my sensitivity and empathy for each of us as we chart our unique paths. I know fear and love alike wear many masks, has many names, and takes all kinds of forms. As I sat to meditate on how I'd like to conclude this book, I sat with my eyes closed, and immediately opened them to grab my notebook. I wasn't evaluating, or analyzing. I drew no conclusions. This is what I wrote:

I am not having an identity crisis.
I am a dichotomy.
That is who I am.
I am as malleable as an ice cube on my tongue.
I am both freezing and melting.

Very few of us are either evil or angelic.
But we have all seen the dense black of night and
squinted in the blinding light of the sun.
We are all a bit good.
And bad.
For that, I have no shame.
Nor pride.
I am ecstatic and melancholy.
My life has purpose and is senseless.
I delight in wonder and I'm frustrated I know so
very little.
I am confident.
And fucking terrified.
I am elegant.
And I just swore like a sailor.
I trust myself.
Second guess myself.
Move forward.
And inch back.
If I were to scroll up I would want to change what
I've written.
Because I'm different now.
I'm old.
Or getting older.
But every second is new.

I've never been here before.
I am discovering who I am.
When I figure it out
I'll inform you.
But by then we both will have sneezed.
Or blinked.
Hurt.
Or been pained.
One or both of us would have found something
funny.
Or felt irate.
And for all those reasons
You would hear me differently.
And by the time I finished.
I will have changed.

A part of me wishes I could conclude this book in complete faith that we've exhausted all the ways fear tries to stunt us. That we've unpacked and dismantled fears ability to haunt us. The most idealized and romantic part of me wants to believe that the woes of fears will be fables that live on only through the stories we'll one day share with our grandkids. That kids will all huddle around captivated and intrigued by the concept of fear because it'll seem as outdated as dial-up or polio. No longer an inconvenience or threat. I want to say I've eradicated fear in my life. That I no longer shrink near an army of egos. Oh how pleasant it might be to wrap this book in a cleanly tied ribbon and pretend fear will never make a mess of any relationship ever again. But another part of me is grateful for fear because it gives us incentive to shift perspectives and strengthen that which opposes it. The truth is that fear will continue to be a source of bewilderment. While fear may not be ephemeral, I know for certain, love is eternal. I trust that we all have the ability to love and be loved. I know that we are worthy of love, and no circumstance can strip us of that. I'm certain of very little, but I know this much, the love we have for ourselves is as much our birthright as it is our gift. I'll end with this quote from Maya Angelou, "I don't trust people who don't love themselves, but say I love you."

REFERENCES

Attached

Pinguin Random House LLC

2011

375 Hudson Street, New York, NY 10014

www.attachedthebook.com

A Course in Miracles

New Christian Church of Full Endeavor, Ltd.

2007

P.O.Box 217, Lake Delton, WI 53940

Email: mcc@acimi.com

www.acimi.com

The Book of Joy

Penguin Random House LLC

2016

375 Hudson Street, New York, NY 10014

Conscious Loving

Bantam Books

1990

Conscious Uncoupling

Harmony Books, division of Penguin Random House

2015

Daring Greatly

Penguin Books Ltd

2012

www.Brenebrown.com

The Four Agreements

Amber-Allen Publishing

2010

www.thefouragreements.com

The Gift of Change

Harper One

2004

www.harpercollins.com

www.marianne.com

Power vs. Force

Hay House

1995

www.spiritualteachers.com/david-hawkins/

Sapiens

Harper

2015

195 Broadway, New York, NY 10007

Secrets for Success and Inner Peace

Hay House

2016

www.drwaynedyer.com

21 Lessons for the 21st Century

Spiegel & Grau, Random House

2018

youtube.com/c/YuvalNoahHarari1

Why You're Not Married Yet

Ballantine Books

2013

www.tracymcmillian.com

The Yoga Sutras of Patanjali

Penguin Random House

ABOUT THE AUTHOR

KRISTEN SCHNEIDER IS a three time author, international yoga teacher, board certified Ayurveda Practitioner, and world traveler. She studies and practices Eastern philosophy and medicine. She currently lives in Tampa, Florida.

CPSIA information can be obtained
at www.ICGtesting.com
Printed in the USA
FSHW011532151120
75840FS